*Fiercely represent a*

# Fierce

# &

# Fearless

**Rochelle C. Guiton**

# Fierce & Fearless

Copyright © 2021 by Rochelle C. Guiton
All rights reserved.
Printed in the United States of America.
ISBN (PAPERBACK): 978-1-7366022-0-1
ISBN (HARDCOVER): 978-1-7366022-1-8
ISBN (EBOOK): 978-1-7366022-2-5
ISBN (WORKBOOK): 978-1-7366022-3-2
Published by Edward, Elva, and Gerry (EE&G) Publishing Company
God's Spoiled Brats, LLC
www.GodsSpoiledBrats.com
Edited by Create and Blossom, LLC
Cover art by Create and Blossom, LLC
Layout by One Creative HTX
Photographs by Kelly Hornberger

Also used: THE HOLY BIBLE, NEW INTERNATIONAL VERSION®,
NIV® Copyright © 1973, 1978, 1984, 2011 by Biblica, Inc.™ Used by
permission.
All rights reserved worldwide.
Also used: Scripture taken from the New King James Version®. Copyright
© 1982 by Thomas Nelson, Inc. Used by permission. All rights reserved.
Also used: Scripture quotations are taken from the Holy Bible, New Living
Translation, copyright © 1996, 2004, 2007 by Tyndale House Foundation.
Used by permission of Tyndale House Publishers, Inc., Carol Stream, IL
60188. All rights reserved.
Also used: "Scripture quotations are from the ESV® Bible (The Holy Bible,
English Standard Version®), copyright © 2001 by Crossway, a publishing
ministry of Good News Publishers. Used by permission. All rights
reserved."

Also used: King James Version which is public domain

GOD'S *Spoiled* BRATS     EE&G
EDWARD ELVA & GERRY
PUBLISHING

Jacquelin

It great to meet you and I can not wait to partner up I know we will

Pierce

*For girls, teenagers, young and adult women struggling with balancing the pressures of the world and fulfilling her true God given purpose. God hears you and is here for you.*

# Dedication

*To my parents, Laura and Tyrone Cooper, my grandparents, Edward and Elva LeBeauf, and Geraldine Keys, whose sound, diligent prayers I am still living out today, tomorrow, and forever.*

*Charm is deceptive and beauty is fleeting,*
*But a woman who fears the Lord, she*
*shall be praised.*

*Proverbs 31:30 NIV*

# Table of Contents

# Acknowledgements

It's not often that people rally around to support so wholeheartedly. I've always had guidance from God in the form of family, friends, and my sisters in Christ. Every one of you knows exactly who you are and have done so without fail. I'm grateful to everyone in my village. Especially grateful for the prayers, encouragement, and motivation from my life group, God's Jewels. I hope Fierce and Fearless blesses every person reading it, as writing it has immeasurably blessed me. I hope my heart, my love, my hugs, and most of all, God's love, are felt through every page you read.

# Introduction

*How many of us are willing to admit that
we are complete spoiled brats?*

Even more, the question is, how did we become such spoiled brats? We live in a world that provides most necessities at the tap of a finger, like on our phone or on our computer. We want what we want at the speed of lightning. Sometimes, there's a specific item that we want from a store, and the item becomes unavailable. Or we have been working hard studying for a test, and did not do as well as we expected. Most of us would be upset about this, and maybe even cry. We would be discouraged. If the "want" was important enough to us, we may have sank into a depression. This is a normal response. We all have emotional responses to disappointments. But, what if there was another way out of the darkness of letdowns and into a life that allowed you to be content, even in a catastrophe? A life that allowed you to be a spoiled brat, but one with a mission and purpose – God's Spoiled Brat.

What happens when you don't get what you want? How do you respond when you don't get what you want? Are you allowing the desires of material things to dictate how you live?

Have you ever wanted to make the rules, decide when, where and how your life would happen? Have you ever thought, even at ten, twelve, maybe even thirteen years old, that you were ready to be an adult? Just lying in bed in your room dreaming that you could leave the stresses of your teenage life, the weight of your parents' rules, and be an adult for just one day, may sound good. Surely, you have spent time imagining your future independence and thought, this would make your life better if you just had one less person telling you what to do and how to do it because you already have all the answers. Believe it or not, everyone has felt this way at some point in their lives.

Some of you are unfortunately living lives full of anger, disappointment, regrets, sadness, and despair, at least until you figure out how you can go from a whiny brat to the confident woman you desire to be, the woman that God wants you to be. And certainly, if God is who He says He is, He can show each of us who He wants us to be. We have watched enough television, movies, reality shows. What the world wants is no longer working. As you try to fit in with modern society, you will quickly learn that you cannot please everyone. And, because you are not being authentic, true to yourself and your purpose, you are unhappy. So why not try it God's way?

This book is an exploration into who God wants us as young girls and women to be.

This book is a journey to God, a constantly evolving and growing relationship with Him. If you take anything away from this book, let it be that God will always be what you need when you need Him. Whether you write letters to him like I did, cry out to him in prayer, or have a simple conversation with Him, He will provide your needs.

I've included some of my journals in this book that will demonstrate how I wrote to God, how I called Him, and when and about what I needed at that specific time. When you need peace, call out to Yahweh Shalom (The Lord is Peace). When you need His power, cry out to El Shaddai (God Almighty). No matter what your basic need or desire is, the same consistent God will shine through and show up during your desperate moments. I know this because He showed up for me. The same God will show up and shine just for you; without fail, without judgment, and always on time if you give Him the opportunity. He will do this no matter how young, how old, inexperienced, or out of touch you are with Him. This is true throughout all our ever-evolving attempts at being the women that God wants us to be.

There are realities that come with being a woman in general, and then we face the added pressures of balancing the goals that are set by society and those steps that are ordered by God. This is a lot of pressure on a grown woman, and so much more pressure on a younger woman. And because we have a lot of added pressure on us, we put more pressure on God to provide all our wants, desires, and of course, our needs.

You must ask yourself, "How did I become such a spoiled brat?" Not a spoiled brat in the sense of an annoying, nagging, crying child who screams at the top of her lungs until she gets what she wants. Not meaning a spoiled brat like an unpleasant little monster child that no one, not even grandma, wants to babysit. Spoiled Brat meaning modern society's craving to receive and obtain material possessions, achieve personal success constantly, and desire of social acceptance. Some of us fully believe and know Christ, but we get so upset and feel abandoned by God when things do not go as planned. It's this idea that we are entitled to everything that we want, exactly when we want it. What's the saying, "If you want to hear God laugh, tell Him your plans." This still holds true. And it doesn't mean, if Plan A doesn't work that you give up, it just means move on to Plan B. The closer you grow in God; you will learn that God wants us to be happy where we are before He elevates us.

And those that don't know Christ, whether you want to or not, there is a word or two in here for you as well. There is no harm in giving God a try. If nothing else, His principles are rooted in good moral character and sound wisdom. And no doubt, every female could use a little advice on how to better juggle, multitask, reason, and balance all the things we as women are expected to handle with ease. Because let's be honest, while men hold extremely important roles in our society, it's the women that often influence, organize, and maintain all the intricate pieces that the men forget. Women are often working two times harder, longer, and faster to get the job, the respect, and the acknowledgement.

When we want something, we quickly fall on our knees in prayer and supplication, pleading with God to aid us in our various vain attempts to get what we want. We repeat selfish prayers for our personal gain. This yearning to succeed is so inherent that we put all other important matters aside to achieve what we consider greater victories. And even though we are immensely blessed, we find excuse after excuse as to why we should not go to church or Bible study. "I'm tired," "I'll go next week," "It's boring," "It's only for adults." We get so wrapped up in our individual needs that we miss opportunities to show others around us Christ's love. And yet we know God and what He is all about.

God, the merciful Father that He is, mostly fulfills our request. Yet, at the least hint of a shortcoming like bad grades on a report card, mom doesn't want to buy those shoes we wanted, or the cute guy in school likes someone else, we become hard-hearted towards God for not responding to our request. It's as if we rub the genie's lamp and magically want God to give us what we wished. If only God was a genie in a bottle.

Sometimes our request are not only material desires in life. As women, we are often troubled by our appearance as well. Each of us wish we looked like someone else, was thinner, prettier, had shorter hair, longer hair, or whiter teeth. We turn to other women on television, music videos, and reality shows to tell us what we should look like, aspire to be, and even act like. Unfortunately, measuring ourselves by modern societies standards will never allow us to reach the full potential of what God says is excellence.

What qualities is God looking for? Well that's where we are going to start. How do we know what qualities are important to God? Where does God want us to focus? What should dictate how we live our lives? Whose lead should we follow? And why on earth with so many other examples, should we be led by the Bible? When a woman is feeling down on herself, down about life, where can she look to build her confidence and outlook on life?

Life is challenging, especially for teenagers. Everyone tells you what to do. You battle influences and peer pressure all around you. You have a desire to fit in, to be liked, to be popular, and try to balance this with following the rules and guidelines at home and school. The difficulty in not fitting in with the crowd, can cause enough anxiety to last a lifetime.

Each day of high school, you look in your closet staring at all the clothes that you picked out and wonder which is the coolest. And if it's not cool enough, you'll throw it out while wishing you could have a brand new wardrobe. Well, a new wardrobe would be nice no matter what, right? Every woman everywhere agrees with this! But one day, you picked those clothes out and they were perfect for you! So why do you have to change to be like everyone else? Don't you know that God created you to be special and unique for a reason? One day, He will need you to stand up on your own distinct platform and effectuate change the way only you could accomplish change. He will need you to be the virtuous woman each of us are called to be in our own way.

In Proverbs Chapter 31, God tells us exactly what it takes to be a virtuous woman. Take it slow when reading it for the first time. It can be intimidating; however, it is an accurate depiction of the woman we should all aspire to be every single day. The responsibilities of the virtuous woman are voluminous and tiring, but she never resigns to failure. Never.

Proverbs is a book in the Old Testament of the Bible, and it is known for bringing attention to good values, acceptable behavior, and the importance of having wisdom. Resonating throughout the chapters of Proverbs is the philosophy that fearing God is the beginning of wisdom, something we can never have too much of. Fearing God, meaning giving God respect, honor, reverence, is the start of gaining wisdom. And this kind of knowledge, you must truly seek to earn the discernment and intellect that God can provide. Chapter 31, the last chapter of Proverbs, starts with lessons to a king from his mother, and then further in verses 10-31, provides an intricate description of the ideal wise woman. Besides just being beautiful poetry, it profoundly offers insight into the complete virtuous woman.

### *A Wife of Noble Character*

*Who can find a virtuous and capable wife?*
*She is more precious than rubies.*
*Her husband can trust her,*
*and she will greatly enrich his life.*
*She brings him good, not harm,*
*all the days of her life.*
*She finds wool and flax*
*and busily spins it.*
*She is like a merchant's ship,*
*bringing her food from afar.*
*She gets up before dawn to prepare breakfast for her household*
*and plan the day's work for her servant girls.*
*She goes to inspect a field and buys it;*
*with her earnings she plants a vineyard.*
*She is energetic and strong,*
*a hard worker.*
*She makes sure her dealings are profitable;*
*her lamp burns late into the night.*
*Her hands are busy spinning thread,*
*her fingers twisting fiber.*
*She extends a helping hand to the poor*
*and opens her arms to the needy.*

*She has no fear of winter for her household,*
*for everyone has warm clothes.*
*She makes her own bedspreads.*
*She dresses in fine linen and purple gowns.*
*Her husband is well known at the city gates,*
*where he sits with the other civic leaders.*
*She makes belted linen garments*
*and sashes to sell to the merchants.*
*She is clothed with strength and dignity,*
*and she laughs without fear of the future.*
*When she speaks, her words are wise,*
*and she gives instructions with kindness.*
*She carefully watches everything in her household*
*and suffers nothing from laziness.*
*Her children stand and bless her.*
*Her husband praises her:*
*"There are many virtuous and capable women in the world,*
*but you surpass them all!"*
*Charm is deceptive, and beauty does not last;*
*but a woman who fears the Lord will be greatly praised.*
*Reward her for all she has done.*
*Let her deeds publicly declare her praise.*

*Proverbs 31:10-31 NLT*


It is tedious to think about being a virtuous woman at thirteen years old, but we must start in the right frame of mind. We cannot wait until we are grown, married, with children, and then decide to be a virtuous woman. We must start now. The question is, how do you start? Proverbs Chapter 31 is a lot to take in. If we go line by line, it is overwhelming. You mean to tell us that God wants women to stay up late, burning the midnight oil to care for the household and wake up before sunrise? In addition to that, he wants us to buy the land, grow the fruit, make the clothes, make wise financial decisions, and care for our husband, on and on and on? We can get tired just thinking about it. You can hardly care for yourself at the age of 13 much less the entire household. And He expects us to do this without any sleep? And we thought women needed their beauty rest. At some point, children and work get added in. What an overwhelming amount of responsibility.

Don't read Proverbs 31 in a vacuum. Each line taken separately and apart is scary, even frightening. It seems no one we know could live up to that standard. It sounds like perfection. Who is this woman that hardly sleeps, is loved by her husband, respected by everyone, talented, wise, and let it not go unnoticed that she only "opens her mouth in wisdom?" So, she's not getting any sleep and can hold her tongue, meaning, she does not argue, is not sassy, and does not gossip. You may not admit it, but some of us struggle with staying calm in anger. Who can hold their tongue? Who can control their attitude? What's your attitude like when you're tired? And this woman, this woman of God is immersed in tiring work.

Consider reading Proverbs Chapter 31 with the entire picture in mind. Think about what it means to be virtuous. If you described someone as virtuous, the person would have high moral standards, be righteous, and upright. You would describe all the characteristics that we expect in any good woman. The truth is, we don't have to wait until we have our own home and family to begin to practice the excellence that God has called us to do in Proverbs 31. We can start the life of a virtuous woman today. Take the fact that she is married and has children completely out of the scenario. What can we learn from her? What kind of person is she? Why is she so valued?

She is hardworking, reliable, and compassionate. She is never idle and never waste time. She makes every moment matter, and she cherishes her time.

We should get excited when we think of a virtuous woman, much like, when we think of our favorite celebrity. Some of our favorite celebrities are women who have either played characters in shows or movies that are virtuous women. It's amazing because God has written it in such a way that every one of us can be her. Stop and think about this for a few minutes. Imagine the full-grown virtuous woman you dream of becoming. As adults, we can imagine this modestly, classic, and yet noticeably remarkable woman that captures everyone's attention.

Imagine her around the Christmas season. It's one of the busiest seasons of the year. She works a full-time job, is married, has three school aged children, maintains hobbies, has trustworthy friendships, and is active in church. Her name is Vee. She's savvy, educated, enthusiastic, witty, and a wholesome, down-home unpretentious woman. She has a way of attracting attention without overtly asking for it, but people consistently flock to her and listen when she speaks. She has perfect stability throughout all her life. Her work, her home, husband, children, hobbies, and church life are all well planned with love, strength, and honor. There is not a soul that has met her that hasn't aspired to be more like her. She encourages other women to be their own perfect examples of high moral character in their own lives. She has become a professional at guarding her tongue and expressions, until it is the ideal time to speak, if even at all. Vee is the light of all the Christmas parties. She turns heads from men and women alike, as she eloquently walks into a room. Her relationship with God radiates out of her like sunlight, so much so, that her smile allows others to feel loved. She shines in a way, not that others want to be her, but that they want to know what she knows, they want to feel what she feels. And of course, if asked or motioned to speak by the Spirit to tell her wisdom, she will respond that she is praised because she fears only God. She doesn't leave the room, until she has touched each person, with kindness, strength, or a good deed.

So, how did Vee become Virtuous Vee. How does Vee maintain and balance all of life's scenarios, without falling short of her goals? Well, she knows God and has a relationship with Him. How do we get to know God and have a relationship with Him? How do we ensure that we influence the young women around us? How do we shine like Vee shines? No, it's not easy. But Vee has captured some things in areas that we all should develop. Even in her own struggles, she made time to influence and encourage other women. She builds God's Kingdom by inspiring and growing the sisterhood. Vee fiercely represents and fearlessly trust in God. And to represent and trust, you must start very simply by reading the Bible, where God shares His heart for women.

# Journal

Dear Yahweh Rohi (The Lord is my Shepherd, Psalm 23:1-3),

I was seven or eight years old when I learned the 23rd Psalm. Aside from the Lord's Prayer, it was the only other part of the Bible I had memorized at that age. My Uncle Warren on one random hot summer day, told me to memorize it. I remember wondering why my uncle wanted me to memorize this old poem. It made absolutely no sense to me at all, at least not at that time. Unsurprisingly, I now often meditate on those words to find comfort from You. I've never forgotten it; not a single word. My favorite part, "yea, though I walk through the valley of the shadow of death, I will fear no evil; For You are with me." As a child, I didn't get the depth of those words. Eventually, when I did memorize every word, I was proud of myself; but only proud in a sense that I had accomplished a small goal. I memorized it much like a song or a nursey rhyme. Over time, as my relationship with you grew, I recognized it, as the exact way You walk beside me. Reading and saying it has more meaning now. You were holding me for every tear I cried, you heard every prayer, and each hardship that shaped me, you were leading me in the path of righteousness. God was creating a path for me to shine on to the next obstacle. When my uncle had me learn the 23rd Psalm back then, I thought the Bible was for adults. I didn't even invest the time to see or appreciate that You were ready and waiting for me the whole while. And just like you waited for me, you are waiting on so many others. Every woman, and little woman alike, should know Your love. So grateful for Your patience. So ready to get to know You better.

Love,

God's Spoiled Brat

*The Lord is my shepherd; I shall not want.*
*He maketh me to lie down in green pastures:*
*He leadeth me beside the still waters.*
*He restoreth my soul: He leadeth me*
*in the paths of righteousness for his name's sake.*
*Yea though I walk through the valley of the shadow of*
*death, I will fear no evil: for thou art with me; Thy rod*
*and thy staff they comfort me.*
*Thou preparest a table before me in the presence of*
*mine enemies: thou annointest my head with oil; my*
*cup runneth over.*
*Surely goodness and mercy shall follow me all the days*
*of my life: and I will dwell in the house of the Lord*
*forever.*

*Psalm 23 KJV*

# CHAPTER ONE

## God is Not Just for Mom and Dad

The Bible isn't just for Mom and Dad. So, why aren't more of us as young Christians getting connected with God? Why aren't we using the wisdom of God in our decision making throughout all our lives? If we are not connecting with God, we are missing the big picture. In fact, we are missing the most important one, the opportunity of eternal life with God. Securing eternal life with God is done by proclaiming Him as your Lord and Savior, living with Him, and by having a relationship with Him. Neither Mom and Dad, Aunt, Uncle, Sister, Brother can stand in your place and do this for you.

Reading and studying the Bible is the best way to know God. In fact, it is the only way to get to know God. Don't get bogged or rather weighted down with what you don't understand. The first thing we must do is stop making excuses, and saying we don't understand the Bible, or that we do not have access to one. In fact, there are tons of free Bibles online and free Bible applications for cell phones, iPads, and tablets. Many churches give away Bibles to new members. Bibles are just as easily accessible as anything else on the internet. It is literally a quick internet search away. Besides, you can't beat getting a free book, right?! The next step would be to try different versions of the Bible. The Bible comes in several different languages. There is a Bible for everyone. Although, they come in different languages and versions, they share the exact same principles and teachings. Find one you really like and invest in yourself. Get your own hard copy of the Bible as soon as you can afford one.

Your Bible may also have some commentary or annotations to help. It must be a version of the Bible that you can understand or grow to understand. This is going to vary depending on your style of reading and studying. Always start your reading with prayer. Pray for wisdom and understanding and specifically ask the Holy Spirit to illuminate the scriptures and give you revelation. Put in the work and study, prayerfully and allow the Holy Spirit to lead you.

*Do your best to present yourself to God as one approved, a worker who does not need to be ashamed and who correctly handles the word of truth.*

*2 Timothy 2:15 NIV*

Getting a Bible is an investment in yourself. We all must invest in ourselves and building your relationship with God is exactly that. How can you make decisions about what you want, love, and need, without knowing yourself and who you are in Christ? Reading the Bible

18

teaches you who you are in God and through God. Your life will change when you learn what God says about you. And then you can embrace it and live the way He teaches us to live.

It is easy to get lost in your own thoughts, to get confused, or even worse to accept the negativity and stereotypes around us. Modern society feeds a lot into our minds that cause all of us to be more concerned with material things or worldly things.

But when you build your relationship with God, you will become so much closer to Him. You will want Him to be a part of every decision you make and conversation you have. You will want to know what He thinks, how he would handle every situation, and most importantly need His direction. But you see this doesn't come from intuition, this comes from reading the Bible and getting to know God. So, when the time comes for you to hear that small, sweet voice, you will know it is Him because you recognize Him. You will have carried Him in your heart for so long, there is no doubt that it is Him. You will know His voice and feel His loving presence.

God wants us to have nice things and God wants us to have a good life. He does not want us to replace knowing Him and knowing how to show love because we think God is only for grown-ups. The best way to make sure that you are living a life focused on God and what God wants for you is to be more intentional about your day-to-day life. Being intentional means, you must spend time thinking about what to do with your time to be productive. You must spend time with God. Reading your Bible will provide direction to your daily life. It will intentionally build a deep-rooted relationship with God, just as you would have with your best girlfriend. You can trust Him with all your secrets. So, how do I get to the deep rooted, intimate relationship with God right now? How do I get there as a young adult, teenager, a student?

Being intentional requires you to slow down. I know you can't slow down time. The actual passing of time is not in our control. Slow down your pace, your thoughts, plan more, and plan efficiently. Get past the surface. Get past the superficial.

Stop simply doing what you think everyone else likes and what everyone else is doing. Look beyond what everyone else designates as cool. If you want to conquer a dream or reach a goal, get determined. Do not waver. Go to God in prayer, write down your goals, and strategize with God to learn ways you can accomplish this goal together. There is no need to be insincere, shallow, or phony about your desires, your likes and dislikes. Be true and authentic to who you are inside. We don't need a world full of robots following the social norms and Instagram fads. God needs bold, courageous women ready to conquer their dreams. God needs women who aren't afraid of failing and falling short every now and then. Take every dream, goal, and desire to God in prayer, during your intentional, private time with Him.

Just as you trust Him with your ambitions, you can also pray to Him about your disappointments and frustrations. However, don't allow those things to bring down your spirits. Your relationship and trust in God should lift you up. God did not put us here on this earth to cry over spilled milk. He did not put us here to loiter away our time being depressed over things that are out of our control. Our happiness should not come from whether our friends think we have on stylish clothing. Our happiness comes from knowing we can do anything through Christ.

*Not that I was ever in need, for I have learned how to be content with whatever I have. I know how to live on almost nothing or with everything. I have learned the secret of living in every situation, whether it is with a full stomach or empty, with plenty or little. For I can do everything through Christ, who gives me strength.*

*Philippians 4: 11-13 NLT*

Let those words resonate in your mind. You can do anything through Christ. It does not say you will always get what you want, but you will get through anything with Him. Even if you fail, God will pull you through. In other words, He will provide you with the contentment you need to win or lose. You can live with almost nothing or with everything with Christ. You have the secret to making it amidst any and every situation. When your stomach is full or empty, you can be content. Whether you make the dance team or not, you can be content, but only with Christ, who gives you the strength you need to withstand. When we get bogged down with circumstances and life is not going our way, remember, God did not give His only Son so that we could spend our days constantly wishing our days were better. God loved the world so much that He gave His only Son, so that whoever believed in Him would have eternal life. John 3:16 NLT

The Bible says "whoever" believes in Him. There is no specific one type of person. It does not say, wait until you are an adult, married, or are parents. It does not say only "old people" can believe. And know this, believing in Him, doesn't just mean you think He exists. It is a heartfelt trust in His way and His will. It is faith that God did, does and will do what He promises. It is studying His word, engraving it in your heart, and living it. And if you are living as God says and as Jesus did; well, there is no time for superficial. You won't even have time to shed tears over a lost popularity contest. You will not have time to cry over lost friends who never treated you the way you deserve to be treated. When you engulf yourself in God, you will find yourself getting deeper into things that truly matter in life. You'll care more about building true friendships, caring for the people and community around you, and spreading all the good news you know about Christ. You will be amazed at how much more fulfilling your life will be. The words in Philippians 4:11-13 will be so evident to you. Your happiness will come from a place of knowing where your help comes from, and the satisfaction in pleasing God.

When you know God through having a relationship with Him, your negative thoughts will decrease. Instead of having contempt for God because he didn't respond when you rubbed on His genie lamp, you recognize His love is about much more than magically responding to each "bratty" request and gesture. His love is about service and when you serve Him, He will honor you. When you are having a bratty moment remember these scriptures.

*Anyone who wants to serve me must follow me, because my servants must be where I am. And the Father will honor anyone who serves me.*

*John 12:26 NLT*

You serve God when you align yourself with the purpose's He has set out for you. And just like scripture gives guidance on service to God, He also provides scripture to help us in everything else. Scripture even provides us with the weapons we need for protection. Ephesians 6:10-20 not only describes your weapons when you need protection, but this scripture shows us how God's word will be our defense in our time of need.

*A final word: Be strong in the Lord and in his mighty power. Put on all of God's armor so that you will be able to stand firm against all strategies of the devil. For we are not fighting against flesh-and-blood enemies, but against evil rulers and authorities of the unseen world, against mighty powers in this dark world, and against evil spirits in the heavenly places. Therefore, put on every piece of God's armor so you will be able to resist the enemy in the time of evil. Then after the battle you will still be standing firm. Stand your ground, putting on the belt of truth and the body armor of God's righteousness. For shoes, put on the peace that comes from the Good News so that you will be fully prepared. In addition to all of these, hold up the shield of faith to stop the fiery arrows of the devil. Put on salvation as your helmet, and take the sword of the Spirit, which is the word of God. Always pray in the Spirit and on every occasion. Stay alert and be persistent in your prayers for all believers everywhere. And pray for me, too. Ask God to give me the right words so I can boldly explain God's mysterious plan that the Good News is for Jews and Gentiles alike. I am in chains now, still preaching this message as God's ambassador. So, pray that I will keep on speaking boldly for him, as I should.*

*Ephesians 6:10-20 NLT*

But remember you can't use those powerful scriptures at the right time unless you know them and what they mean. With reading scripture comes power, knowledge, and understanding. It will strengthen your prayers and prayer life. If you don't know what to pray, ask the Holy Spirit to lead you.

Scriptures like this one will begin to come to life as you rely on the Holy Spirit to help you through prayer.

*In the same way, the Spirit helps us in our weakness. We do not know what we ought to pray for, but the Spirit himself intercedes for us through wordless groans. And he who searches our hearts knows the mind of the Spirit, because the Spirit intercedes for God's people in accordance with the will of God.*

*Romans 8:26-27 NIV*

*If you love Me, keep My commandments. And I will pray the Father, and He will give you another Helper, that He may abide with you forever— the Spirit of truth, whom the world cannot receive, because it neither sees Him nor knows Him; but you know Him, for He dwells with you and will be in you. I will not leave you orphans; I will come to you. A little while longer and*

24

*the world will see Me no more, but you will see Me.*
*Because I live, you will live also. At that day you will*
*know that I am in My Father, and you in Me, and I in*
*you. He who has My commandments and keeps them, it*
*is he who loves Me. And he who loves Me will be loved*
*by My Father, and I will love him and manifest Myself*
*to him.*

*John 14:15-21*

You will get the profound connection to Christ, by loving Christ. Believing isn't enough. Going to church is not enough. You must know Christ for yourself. You must live like Christ.

Relying on mom and dad will not get you into heaven. Relying on grandma's prayers will not be enough. Grandma, mom, dad, auntie, pastor, all had a personal and private relationship with God, and intimately got to know Christ on their own. Give yourselves the same pleasure of knowing, loving, and communing with God. God is not just for mom and dad.

# CHAPTER TWO

## The Struggle ... Don't Sweat the Small Stuff

You know life is hard enough without each of us behaving like vultures. We slowly eat away at each other's spirits, by being obsessed with who dresses the best, shops at the best stores, and what music is trending. And let's not even add the vanity that social media has created. Instead of just sharing special moments with family and friends, we spend time saying this picture looks terrible, after trying five different camera filters. Let's take ten more pictures, until the angle from the chin is just right. Hey, don't deny it, we all do it before we post our pictures. After posting, we scroll through everyone else's timeline and compare their lives to our lives. Who got to go on the best vacations, went to the best parties, took the best family pictures.

Everyone has a point in their lives when they feel like an outsider. Maybe you don't feel like the coolest person, the best dressed, or the most well-liked person.

But people change daily. One day you're at the bottom wondering how you fell, and the next day you're on top, lavishing in happiness. The problem is, when you're on the top, you forget what it was like to be on the bottom. No one talks about being on the bottom. So, when you're there, it's lonely. Instead of sharing with friends or family who care about us, we tend to sulk to ourselves; too embarrassed to discuss it, too ashamed to admit it, and way too sad to just move on. Everyone has been there before. No one likes it, so let's change and help each other deal with the lows in life. Besides, we are stronger together. Given that we all share a lot of the same struggles, we already have an unspoken bond, a sisterhood of likeness. Why not help each other, instead of hurting one another.

Life is not about material things and popularity. Life is about relationships. We need relationships with God and the people around us, especially other women for support. When you are at the top and you peer down at someone in the middle of a struggle, don't scoff at them. Don't look down at them in disdain. Look eye level with compassion and be ready to lend a hand to pull them up with you. Let your sister know, "This happened to me too, and this is how I got through it," or "This is what our God can do for you too." This is how we overcome together.

*And they have defeated him by the blood of the Lamb and by their testimony. And they did not love their lives so much that they were afraid to die.*

*Revelation 12:11 NLT*

The earlier you build your relationship with God, the more wisdom and perspective you will gain to help you deal with what's ahead. You can miss out on so much by concentrating on the small stuff like worrying about what people think, or what people will say. Earlier, I mentioned how the pressures of teen life are difficult. It makes it hard or in the least bit scary to stand out and choose for yourself. The fear of not fitting in can be paralyzing; so paralyzing that you are not able to think what you want for yourself, what makes you happy. The truth is, building your life with God can help you grow past any paralyzing fear and into the wisdom God so desperately wants to share with us.

As I mentioned before, God is not a genie in a bottle. You can't rub the outside of a bottle and have God jump out in a cloud of smoke to grant your every wish. In fact, we should find happiness in knowing that God doesn't give us everything we want all the time. Sometimes, the things that we want are not good for us, and most times we are clueless to what we really need. Of course, hindsight often helps us to see the truth of our situation after it happens. We can then see it from all angles. God, on the other hand, lives in hindsight. His understanding is all encompassing. So, just think about what would happen if we allow God to take the lead in every decision we make. It would be like having the gift of hindsight, without having to go through the situation.

I had an extremely difficult experience when I was in law school. Prior to what happened, good grades came extremely easy to me. I studied and worked hard without much difficulty. I loved going to school. I loved learning. I started law school bright eyed, enthusiastic, and ready to work. I was accepted into my dream school with a scholarship. I was full of hope that all my dreams would be fulfilled. In my second week of law school, while attending college in New Orleans, Louisiana, Hurricane Katrina made landfall. Thankfully, with the help of my parents, I had the means to evacuate, until the hurricane had passed. Like many others, I hopped in the car, still bright eyed and excited about law school. Considering that many of us in New Orleans doubted the vast effect of Hurricane Katrina, we didn't leave with much. I packed a small bag of clothing and took every one of my books and my laptop with me. I had so many large books they couldn't all fit in a backpack, so I loaded them in a large laundry basket. I thought, "I have to continue studying so that I would be prepared when I returned to school." I can recall the interstate being jammed with traffic, but I studied the entire way to a hotel in Houston, Texas. As I studied, I thought this hurricane would be no different from others I had been through, which had caused minimal harm for my family.

When reality hit, it was all over the news on television in our small hotel room. I saw my street sign nearly covered in water. The water was just low enough for me to read the green sign. I was barely familiar with the sign, considering I had only moved into a brand-new home three months before the flood. Hurricane Katrina was shattering to us all. As I sobbed for hours, for the city of New Orleans and all others affected, we wondered how we could ever recover. This was a tough blow. The beautiful, diverse, culture filled city of New Orleans nearly completely underwater. Such widespread ruin and deadly devastation. Many lost everything they owned, including loved ones, and were forced to rebuild and piece their lives back together from whatever rubble was left behind.

I was heartbroken. I incessantly sobbed, to the point of being physically ill. Even though I was sitting in a dry, warm hotel room I was so wrapped up in my material loss, that I failed to see the value in the gifts that remained. I worried that all I had left was this tiny bag of clothing and a laundry basket full of law school books. I was upset, discouraged, and enraged. How could a hurricane interrupt this dream? What was supposed happen now? Should we give up? How could God allow this to happen?

Thankfully, my parents didn't let me quit. Like many others, I returned to New Orleans with a renewed spirit. It wasn't until after graduating, reaching the finish line, that I would see the growth God would provide me through that experience. The growth, endurance, and tenacity He would allow the entire city of New Orleans to experience and show the world. Sure, it was overwhelming. Sure, we were all filled with self-doubt. Many thinking and believing the hurricane was a sign we should give up or do something else with our lives. To think, that we could be willing to alter an entire dream, our purpose for one problem; albeit it was a major catastrophic one, but one problem, nonetheless. Many of us who experienced Hurricane Katrina carried the depression of this storm throughout our lives.

We can't be engulfed with sadness about any situation, especially if it affects other areas of our lives. While I didn't quit school, I had given up mentally, emotionally, and my grades suffered. I was a complete spoiled brat. I let my dreams fade into the background because of a setback, instead of proving that I could make a comeback. I eventually was able to pull up my grades considerably and graduate, but it was not like I had planned.

I continued to allow myself to feel defeated by the storm and blamed everything on one bad experience. After graduating and passing the bar, I applied for jobs constantly. Again, I had imagined myself in a high paying, high profile job, so those were the positions for which I applied. Unfortunately, my late push for higher grades was not enough. Rejection letters were "the norm" or so I thought. I was down on myself and beating myself up for not having better grades and interviewing skills. And that was only from the responses I received; I had applied for hundreds of jobs. Some of them did not even bother with sending a rejection letter. Well, that was over 10 years ago. Looking at my life back then, and more so, now, no one would ever have known how I struggled. Appearances of success are not always what they seem.

Now, having worked in positions that I love, and in fact, feel called to do, it's easy to see that those hundreds of rejections then, was God's Saving Grace for tomorrow (today). He knew then exactly where He wanted me; exactly where I was needed, exactly where I would feel fulfilled. All that time was spent feeling stressed out, disappointed, and rejected for absolutely no reason at all. God had a better plan.

I'm not saying that I should not have been applying for those jobs and diligently seeking employment. That search helped to find just what God wanted found. Not everyone was in the position to apply for a job, let alone work at all. God alone is responsible for putting us into position to have a college degree, a job, or a promotion in the first place. That in and of itself, is a blessing. So, what's the takeaway from this experience? Fiercely represent and fearlessly trust in God.

It's important to live and love in the now. To be your best where God has you positioned, only then will you be ready to move to the next post He has planned for you. Instead of being down on yourself and feeling unlucky, you should be grateful all the while. Enjoy where God has you positioned and use it to build relationships with God and others. The loss was purely material, but in typical spoiled brat fashion we want God to answer for it all. Why did this have to happen to me?

Just remember in frustrations of failing a test, not fitting in, feelings of not being good enough, God alone sustains us. And He will also strengthen you. Everyone at some point or another has feelings of inadequacy; you are not alone in that. Everyone has problems, failures; you are not alone. The struggles are inherently a part of our growth. And don't sweat the small the stuff, focus on the things that you can control; for example, having a positive attitude and mindset, no matter what the results. Don't waste time harping on the bad thing that happened. Find the silver lining and find happiness in it. God always has plans bigger and better than we could ever imagine.

And here is the amazing part, The Good News, God is with you wherever you go. So, when you take that test, have your first day of high school, trying out for cheerleading or basketball, God is with you. He is with you through failed relationships, lost friends, unemployment, minor setbacks that God will use to build the character you need for your next promotion. Change your focus in those times to scriptures like this one:

*Fear not, for I am with you; Be not dismayed, for I am your God. I will strengthen you, Yes, I will help you, I will uphold you with My righteous right hand.*

*Isaiah 41:10 NKJV*

# CHAPTER THREE

## Who is Really in Control?

Just stop. Stop thinking you can micromanage, manipulate, and dictate every aspect of your lives. We can plot, plan, devise, organize, develop, mold all the intricate facets, but there is only so much we can control. There is a difference between being wise and planning; and believing that we can not only plan our future but know what is best for us ahead. An interrupted or thwarted plan is often God's protection. He knows what's in the future for us. If our blueprint always pans out, we won't ever know when and if God has something bigger purposed for us.

We, as women, often stress over our imperfections. We want to be amazingly perfect at everything. Our appearance, work, school, home, hair... yes, hair becomes so senselessly important. And each day we make attempts to improve our appearance. If we fail at something, anxiety grows and so does stress. And one day, hopefully we finally realize, not only are we stressing about things that were not always in our control, but we were stressing about things that were of no value to God. He just wants us to whole heartedly, with everything in us, serve Him with the gifts and talents He has given us.

So, what does that mean? Fiercely represent and fearlessly trust in God. We still must plan, organize, schedule, but build our faith in the process and pray for guidance from God that He will direct the planning, organizing, and scheduling. The more we involve God in the developing of our lives, the more our lives will be Spirit led, and nourished and blessed by allowing God to lead us. Every step guided by God and therefore protected by him as well.

The Bible tells us that God is our refuge (protection) and our strength. God is always ready to help and most importantly, because of that, we should have no fear when trouble or misfortune arise. Psalm 46 NLT so eloquently tells us that no matter what is going on in the world that God will provide and protect. It goes on to say that God is our fortress.

*The nations are chaos, and their kingdoms crumble.*
*But God's voice thunders and the earth melts.*
*Psalm 46:6 NLT*

There will always be chaos around us. There are unfortunate events in life, crime, violence, physical and sexual abuse. Covid-19 is still plaguing our world, our country, even as I write. These are tough times for everyone on so many levels. It will be years before we all apprehend everything affected by the corona virus. What can we make of it? The sheer volume of lives lost, is mind blowing. As human beings we are aching for the world around us. We are broken hearted on all levels seeing our cities and communities adapt to this dangerous situation, afraid for our lives, concerned about businesses. This is a real life-threatening situation. And in all the darkness of death, isolation, God finds a way to show exactly who He is by allowing His people, the church to maintain even during quarantine. Yes, God is still in control. And just like the rest of world, we adapt. We too have virtual meetings. We too use social media and other resources to continue spreading the Gospel. Now people who only had a little bit of Jesus in church are bringing it right into their living rooms and some who had not gone to church in a long time, there was no longer an excuse. Church is right at their fingertips. Globally God prepared the church just like the rest of the country to adapt, to continue building, to help in the healing.

So, in this fight to save lives, to protect, to create virtual schools, and modify businesses to go remote, God was still in control. In all the typical rapid pace of our lives, juggling school, work, children, sports, and all the things on your plate day to day, God said, let's pause. This epidemic caused us to seclude ourselves, minimize our lifestyles to ordering and shopping for the essentials, become teachers at home to our children, spend more time with family, and get creative about communicating with other people we value. God has shown us in a true pandemic we can adapt, we can trust Him, we can overcome. He has also shown us what fundamentals are truly necessary, who are the people that will be there for us when times get tough, who in all of humanity will have the tenacity to fearlessly fight and stand up for what's right. And lastly, most importantly God said what He has always said in comparable situations, "Be still and know that I am God." Psalm 46:10 NLT

Knowing that God is in control and maintains authority is knowing who God is and what He is capable of. You must trust God. How do you trust someone that you don't know? Well, that's a simple answer. You don't trust someone you don't know. But God tells us exactly who He is, first and foremost in the Bible through scripture, and through us and our experiences. Again, this is how the virtuous woman is so confident in God and therefore in herself. Vee knows that God has authority and dominion over all things and the scripture of Proverbs 31 is carved in her soul. Vee, because she is a virtuous woman, is "energetic and strong" and she must be. Proverbs 31:17 NLT Her successes have not come easy and she had to work for everything. Vee has an unshakable trust in God. Because Vee trust God, her actions show that she has the utmost confidence in the security He provides. His protection exudes through her and she has pride in just simply knowing that God is still on the throne. She is satisfied in knowing that God is truly with her. She gets gratification and comfort from doing all that she can do within her power in any situation and allowing God to do and determine the rest. Vee "laughs without fear of the future." Proverbs 31:25 NLT She has absolutely no fear of the future because she knows God by her side through and through. She has an infectious laugh, so hearty and full that when you hear it, you can almost feel the years of wisdom just saturated in her. Wisdom that she has acquired and invested getting to know God and building her relationship with Him. Her outbursts happen so freely, abrupt, yet so beautiful. Her freedom is in God and nothing else. No other thing or person dictates her boisterous laugh. Not a circumstance, a disappointment, disease, or virus can influence her contentment. She finds her peace and purpose in God.

Sis, we can finish school, get all the educational accolades, eat healthy, exercise, maintain high paying reputable jobs, balance work and family, finances, husband, children, dinner, and last, but not least have great hair, but if we do not know God for ourselves, we will never find peace or purpose. And that, my sister, is a fact. The truth of the matter is, no matter how much we try to juggle all the things, we are still not in control of it all. We are still at the beck and call of life and happen chance, when we "think" we are in control.

But what does the reality of control look like? Imagine you are walking out the door of your apartment on a beautiful Monday morning, a powerful two-piece suit, favorite 3-inch heels, hair done, "nails did," twenty minutes early for an interview at your ideal job. You had an excellent interview. You were able to answer every question with confidence and ease. You leave feeling there is no way you didn't get the job. One week later, you get the standard email back, stating the company has chosen someone else for the position. Instead of moving on, you fantasize what you could have done differently, better to get the job, having forgotten how amazing you felt when you seamlessly answered all their questions. Why do we forget?

Why do we then, because one company didn't select us for the position, forget our worth? The same seems true when we choose an outfit, a restaurant, make a new friend, boyfriend, and one opposing opinion has us second-guessing the instinct we had to like or love those things, and often times ourselves.

The reality is that we cannot control the opinion of others. Too often we think it best that everyone agrees. Even amongst the believers and in church there are going to be variances in belief and understanding. This is normal and should be expected. Unfortunately, differences of opinion inherently cause us to question whether our own feelings, views and ideas are justified. And that is exactly the dilemma, not accepting that our views and opinions are justified without having to be coauthored and adopted by anyone else. Everyone is entitled to their own thoughts and opinions. And remember an idea of perfection is just that, an idea. It's an opinion of one person, not all people. Take comfort in knowing that we are all perfectly imperfect. We should instead take pride in the differences of our opinions and ideas. It is also a part of acknowledging everyone for who they are and where they are in life. The Bible gives us guidance in situations like this.

*Accept other believers who are weak in faith, and don't argue with them about what they think is right or wrong.*
*Romans 14:1 NLT*

God doesn't want us quarreling over opinions and passing judgment on each other. We cannot control those opinions anyway.

*Yes, each of us will give a personal account to God. So let's stop condemning each other. Decide instead to live in such a way that you will not cause another believer to stumble and fall.*

*Romans 14:12-13 NLT*

He wants us to accept each other in love and to use our differences as a source of building relationships and building each other. It will be less about opinions and comparisons. Things that are completely out of your control.

*For the Kingdom of God is not a matter of what we eat or drink, but of living a life of goodness and peace and joy in the Holy Spirit. If you serve Christ with this attitude, you will please God, and others will approve of you, too. So then, let us aim for harmony in the church and try to build each other up.*

*Romans 14: 17-19 NLT*

So, what are some things that are within our control? Well, we can control what we do and say. We control the words that come out of our mouth, the way in which those words are used and said, the tone, the manner, and when they are said. Choosing the right environment for certain conversations can be key to how those tough words are accepted. If we are cornered into having a hard talk with a close friend, we can decide when and where. We can decide when it's best to have a private conversation or a more open one with others present. This we can control and should control.

We can control our self-care; what we eat, our health, and self-maintenance. For some of us it takes a lot of self-discipline, but this is something we can control through the choices we make. There is a distinction between being in complete control and being disciplined. Disciplined is having a controlled set of habits that help you stay organized, more structured, and systematic. It is okay to be disciplined and have a routine. Discipline allows you to create habits and institute order in your life, but with things that are within your control. For example, having a nightly or morning routine to ensure that you get off to school and work timely. This is great preparation for the day. Self-care routines and exercise are a great way to establish heathy habits for a healthy lifestyle. All of this prepares you for normal day to day life, it does not however, mandate that there are no surprises to throw off the routine or that sickness and injury won't interrupt a healthy capable person. Even the most competent, healthy, intelligent people face challenges that they took every measure to avoid. Nonetheless, they took all the precautions, and they did everything correctly and unfortunate, unplanned circumstances of life happened. No matter how great we are, or perfect we seem, we do not hold the power to make certain things happen. The same is so for stopping certain things from happening.

Time and time again we fall apart when those unforeseen events happen. We fall apart out of fear and uncertainty. But you can control how you respond to those circumstances. The emotional responses in anger are never the answer. Let's really think about this, what can we change in anger. What can we change at all? Depending on the situation, maybe nothing within our control. This would be exactly the time to put faith over fear. Recognize that we serve a God that controls all things. When we can't control anything, God can and does control everything.

> *My people will live in peaceful dwelling places,*
> *in secure homes, in undisturbed places of rest.*
> *Isaiah 32:18 NIV*

More problems and disputes are created because of people incorrectly believing they are in control, or moreover, believe that they can and should control others. People believing that they can manipulate. Unfortunately, believing that they can use different tactics to cause a situation to go a certain way. Sometimes it could be using schemes to manipulate people into behaving the way you want them to behave. Or worse, getting angry when someone doesn't respond the way they wanted that person to respond. Some forms of this may come in abusive situations, emotional/verbal abuse, physical, and sexual abuse. This is not how God called us to live. Someone exerting this type of control, manipulation, and abuse is not showing you God's love. They are not showing you the love of Christ that each one of us deserve.

Some abusive situations can leave you feeling or thinking that there is no way out. Maybe you rely on your abuser for financial reasons, maybe you have children together, maybe it's just simply that you love that person and are conflicted about separation. Even in the circumstances of an emotional or mentally abusive situation, know that you are deserving of help. The first thing of significance is knowing that God is a haven for everyone.

*God is our safe place and our strength*
*Psalm 46:1 NLV.*

*He will give you courage when you are afraid.*
*This is my command – be strong and courageous!*
*Do not be afraid or discouraged. For the Lord,*
*your God is with you wherever you go.*
*Joshua 1:9 NLT.*

*He will give you wisdom when you ask for it.*

*If you need wisdom, ask our generous God, and he will*
*give it to you. He will not rebuke you for asking.*
*James 1:5 NLT*

*And those seeking refuge should know that God will*
*protect you. When anyone perpetuates violence or*
*anger, God is not pleased.*

*The Lord examines both the righteous and the wicked.*
*He hates those who love violence.*
*Psalm 11:5 NLT*

*For the righteous Lord loves justice.*

*The virtuous will see his face.*
*Psalm 11:7 NLT*

*The young lions lack and suffer hunger; But those who*
*seek the Lord shall not lack any good thing.*
*Psalm 34:10 NKJV*

*The thief does not come except to steal, and to kill, and to destroy. I have come that they may have life, and that they may have it more abundantly.*

*John 10:10 NKJV*

All of this to say, that God is still God. He will provide what we need. We need not fear for tomorrow and the happening of things not within our control. God has it all handled before we ever know it is a problem. We just need to trust him. And when you trust Him, he will direct you. We can, much like Vee, build our confidence in Him, so that when turmoil hits, we can smile and laugh with a freedom that no thing and no one can take away. In heartbreak, in trouble, even when it looks bleak, even in abusive situations, God hears you. Fiercely represent and fearlessly trust. God in all is power, is in control.

# Journal

Dear Yahweh, Shalom, (The Lord is Peace, Judges 6:24 NKJV),

I remember the day you gave me an idea for this book. It was just after starting this journal, conversations with You. At least now I like to think of them as conversations, back then it was a way to log all my complaints about my life. I was in a deep sleep and suddenly awakened, but I'm not sure how. But it was most definitely You, God. The topic was interjected into my head, as clear as it could be said, God's Spoiled Brat. This book became a mission of mine for years, and unfortunately, for a while, a disappointment. I was angry that You would give me an idea, served it on a silver platter and never provide me with enough time or inspiration to complete it. Over the 10 years that it's taken me to complete this book I have learned; it took time because I was not ready to say what You needed me to say. In fact, I didn't know enough about You or myself to write about it. So here I am 10 years later and 10 years different – not in character, but in strength, dignity, faith, patience, and prayer. Learning to have patience was key in understanding You and accepting Your will for my life. That it was all in Your timing and under Your control. Prayer was imperative to the journey. It was about praying for myself, others, and every situation that came before me. It is about seeking You first. Every one of the readers, has been covered in prayer, all the young girls and women that He desired to reach with this book. What would You have me to tell them? Praying for Your direction in every detail. Desiring to reach every young girl, so that she too could learn to have a relationship with You. Praying for every young woman that would read this book; if she ever doubted herself, her abilities, her beauty. Praying, so that each young woman that reads this book would know that she could come to You with anything. Even if she needed an answer to peer pressure about drugs, alcohol, boys, or just about making good decisions, she knew she could turn to You. When she asked the question, "Am I ready? –for you know what. Don't make me use the word here, you know what I'm talking about. Sex. (insert embarrassed emoji here) All of my friends are doing it. And all the guys want it. I won't have a single friend left that believes in being a virgin and waiting for sex until after marriage." Praying that she knows that You hear every cry, request, and prayer. Praying to You, so You would provide me with the wisdom of just what to tell her here.

Love,

God's Spoiled Brat

# CHAPTER FOUR

## The Answer to Peer Pressure is Easy

The best advice for peer pressure or really any pressure at all, is to pray and ask God for wisdom. In every situation God will provide you with the right answers and the courage to stand by the right convictions. Colossians 1:9 is easily one of my favorite verses. In the mornings on my way to work, my quick morning prayer is God fill me with the knowledge of Your will in all spiritual wisdom and understanding. In times of difficult decisions, which I often face on my job, I say that prayer. Of course, Colossians 1:9 is much more intricate than that, a much more beautiful promise from God. And don't miss that because it is a promise.

*For this reason we also, since the day we heard it, do not cease to pray for you, and to ask that you may be filled with the knowledge of His will in all wisdom and spiritual understanding; that you may walk worthy of*

*the Lord, fully pleasing Him, being fruitful in
every good work and increasing in the
knowledge of God.*
*Colossians 1:9-10 NKJV*

It's twofold. Not only do you pray and ask for
wisdom, but you must increase your knowledge of God.
Increasing your knowledge of God will provide you with
wisdom. The more you read about God, the more you learn
and retain His words and desires. He will give you the ability
to recall straight from your knowledge of Him. You growing
to know God will automatically build your relationship
with Him. Your time with Him will become more like a
conversation, rather than crying out or acting out in rage
when you don't get what you want. When you have a
relationship with God, peer pressure is really no pressure at
all. God is your strength to say no when the answer is no.
God is your influence to say yes or act when you need to
respond a certain way. And know that children and young
adults are not the only people that fight temptations every
day. There are adults that battle persuasions every single
day. Peer pressures can include enticements to do more than
just illegal and seductive things. Peer pressures can come
in the form of commercials to spend money, eat a certain
type of food, to buy a certain car or house. We all have
our own impulses to fight off that often make us weak in
our convictions; our own temptations that make it hard to
do the right thing. However, God will always provide you
with the strength and the wisdom you need to overcome the
weakness or temptation. God did exactly that for Shadrach,
Meshach, and Abednego. Daniel 3:1-30 NKJV
  The King of Babylon, Nebuchadnezzar, made an

image of gold and ordered the people to fall down and worship the gold image when they hear the sound of the horn, flute, harp, lyre, and psaltery (a musical instrument played by plucking strings). He then commanded that anyone who failed to follow his orders would immediately be thrown into a burning fiery furnace. Could you just imagine it, the entire kingdom called to hear the new command of the king? The announcement made formally before all the "satraps, the administrators, the governors, the counselors, the treasurers, the judges, the magistrates, and all the officials of the provinces". Daniel 3:3 NKJV In other words, this announcement was made in front of everyone and all the top, most important officials. The king wanted everyone to take notice and they did. They heard the king's order and as soon as the instruments gave sound, all the people fell and worshiped the gold image designed by King Nebuchadnezzar. But then as everyone else worshiped and fell to their knees it was brought to the king's attention that three men, Shadrach, Meshach, and Abednego did not fall down and worship the gold image as commanded by the king. Of course, this made the king furious. He called the men to him and asked "Is it true that you do not serve my gods or worship the gold image" he had set up. He then asked, "who is the god who will deliver you from my hands." Daniel 3:15 NKJV

You've got to just picture this scene. These three men, who have just defied a command of the king in front of the entire kingdom. The king could not back down from his own orders and allow these three men to not only defy him, but to walk away without repercussions. He had to protect his ego and his image. He had to make sure to make an example out the three of them.

Shadrach, Meshach, and Abednego were facing an insurmountable amount of peer pressure at that time. They could have very easily just given in, followed the kings order, and worshipped the gold image. But they also knew the God they served has commands as well. God's command tells us not to worship idols and to not have any other God before or over him. In the literal heat of the moment before having to walk into a fiery furnace, who's commands were they going to follow?

*And in the most confident, somewhat boastful way, the three men answered "O Nebuchadnezzar, we have no need to answer you in this matter. If that is the case, our God whom we serve can deliver us from the burning fiery furnace, and He will deliver us from your hand, O king. But if not, let it be known to you, O king, that we do not serve your gods, nor will we worship the gold image which you have set up.*
*Daniel 3:16-18 NKJV*

The king, in a rage, ordered his men to heat the furnace seven times more than it is usually heated. He then had the three men bound in their clothing and garments, and then cast out into the furnace. As the men were thrown deep into the fire, he could then see the same three men "walking in the midst of the fire." They were unharmed and they could see four men walking around the fire. King Nebuchadnezzar could do nothing but praise the God of Shadrach, Meshach, and Abednego and he further ordered that "any people, nation, or language" that spoke against Got would be cut into pieces. Daniel 3:29 NKJV

Much like the president's address to the country. The entire country taking notice. An official order and command from the President of the United States of America. There had to have been some great tension in the atmosphere. Every eye on those three meek and modest Jewish men, with nothing but their faith to stand and rely upon. If there are ever any conditions to fall prey to peer pressure, it would most definitely be understood if you gave in under the guise of being thrown into a fiery furnace. Of course, when you think of it that way, it seems a lot easier to say no to drugs and premarital sex. But I totally understand that individual pressures when you are in the moment, no matter how scary, dangerous, or public those pressures are, we all need courage to overcome it.

Shadrach, Meshach, and Abed-Nego refused to give in to the King of Babylon and not only did their faith save them in the fire, but it also influenced Nebuchadnezzar. It made the king a believer as well. You never know when your courage to stand apart from the crowd will inspire others to become believers. You can respond to peer pressure with your own form of the same, but with a positive effect. There is absolutely nothing more constructive than peers teaming together to push each other to do good things. And even further and more encouraging are peers coming together to influence others to serve God. This, my sister, is called discipleship. Discipleship is when you have accepted the principles of God, believe that Jesus died for your sins, and spreading that gospel at every opportunity. If we all stepped up to this, to have this focused influence on the people around us, we would be the leaders God has called us all to be.

Initially, this can be a scary thought. But inherently we all know right from wrong. We know what it feels like to be bullied or picked on. We know we shouldn't be disrespectful of our elders. We know in our hearts that we need to just practice kindness to one another. Having influence and creating positive peer pressures starts with that; doing what you know is right. You feel pressured by others because you want to fit in, but the crowd that wants you to do wrong things, bad things, is not the crowd you want to fit into anyway. They need to feel the pressure to fit in with you. You create the line in the sand that they must cross to be more like you. You dictate the standards that are set to be your friend. And trust me, you are not the only one that feels stigmatized and forced to follow the crowd. There are many others like you, that know when things are wrong but are too afraid to walk into the fiery furnace. I bet if one stood out, maybe you, then others would too and just like Shadrach, Meshach, and Abed-Nego, it could be a trio or crew of Christian sisters walking into the fiery furnace together. Instead of one person saying they won't participate in bullying, using drugs, or premarital sex, it could be an entire group of you creating the new norm of social pressures and positive influences.

You will know the individuals you can trust because they will be the person who is with you when things are down. They are willing to hang out with you at home when you are grounded from the high school party of the year because of bad grades. That person will stand by you when you get teased at school because some popular kid called your shirt ugly in front of the entire class. The person you can trust will be your friend no matter what clothing you have on, grades you make, and because you don't hang out with people who pressure you to break the rules. But without fail, you fiercely represent and fearlessly trust in God. When you are scared or nervous, God will give you the strength you need and a friend or two for support, just like Shadrach, Meshach, and Abed-Nego.

Why do teenagers, for some reason, forget that their parents were once young? I suppose it's never trendy to get advice from your parents. It may not be considered cool, but it most definitely would be wise. I sure would rather get guidance from someone who has lived it and reached the other side of the peer pressure drama, rather than get useless advice from schoolmates that do not have my best interest at heart. Your parents, at some point, were cool, hip, and fashionable. They enjoyed the music of their time, just the same as you. Unfortunately, one day the music you enjoy will be an oldie just the same too.

So how can you show God's love and disciple right where you are in life. Well, the list can be as long as you like. If you have limited means, won't be able to go far from the house; hey, that is okay. Find time to help around the house, do some chores, or help with some necessary repairs. Your parents or guardians will appreciate you, not only because you are assisting around the house, but also because you are doing it out of the goodness of your heart. This will go a long way. It may even inspire your siblings to join in.

Donate your time to your siblings. You can help them with homework or spend time getting to know each other. This is all a part of building relationships; exactly what God wants us to do. Spreading God's love through relationships with others. So many different positive things you can do to build relationships. You can start a bible study group with your friends, talk more openly about God with your friends.

Unfortunately, in our teenage years, we don't realize how important it is to be an individual. How significant it is to stand out, instead of blending in with the crowd or even wanting to be like everyone else. The entire time it stifles what God has in store for you. It seems silly to say this, but you cannot be you, if you are busy trying to be like someone else or everybody else. You cannot stand in the purposes God has for you if you are faking it in someone else's position.

However, if you are continually in tune with the unique individual He wants you to be, could you just imagine how free you would have been in high school and middle school if you didn't worry about what other's thought of how you looked, what you said, how you dressed. How do we get to that point in our thinking? How do we get to the point where we feel free to express how we truly feel, what we really think, to wear what we like, rather than what is in style? Well, the answer is God. Who does God say I am? He tells us exactly who we are in Him and knowing this, gives you a confidence in self, that no one and nothing can take a way.

Who does God want me to be? The good news is that we don't have to go far or guess what kind of woman God wants us to be. He tells us and He's clear in His Word. He speaks directly to each one of us. Yes, in Proverbs Chapter 31 He gives us guidelines, a script of sorts to live up to in caring for our families, friends, in our work, in our relationships, and honor of the Lord.

God, goes even further, and encourages, uplifts, and confirms our value all throughout scripture in the Bible. He so intricately details the worth of women with verses like Psalm 46:5, "God is with her, she will not fail." God literally took the time out to tell us that if He is within us, we WILL NOT fail. He wants us to carry Him with us and value what's on the inside.

*Rather, it should be that of your inner self, the unfading beauty of a gentle and quiet spirit, which is of great worth in God's sight.*
*1 Peter 3:4 NIV*

*Blessed is she who has believed that the Lord would fulfil his promises to her.*
*Luke 1:45 NIV*

Importance of being quiet enough to hear God from within us. The common underlying foundation in all these verses is God. Relationship and trust. Fiercely represent and fearlessly trust.

*No temptation has overtaken you except such as is common to man; but God is faithful, who will not allow you to be tempted beyond what you are able, but with the temptation will also make the way of escape, that you may be able to bear it.*
*1 Corinthians 10:13 NKJV*

In other words, temptations are going to come, but God has already equipped us to escape. He has already given us a way out. This is great news, no matter how big, small, or serious the enticement is, God gives us an exit. We all know we can be tempted by food cravings. How many of us have failed diets? Or said we would only eat so much of something, and then guiltily went back for more? Even in the simplest circumstances of temptation, God will equip us to escape.

*I discipline my body like an athlete, training it to do what it should. Otherwise, I fear that after preaching to others I might be disqualified.*

*1 Corinthians 9:27 NLT*

Your body carries your assignment, your purpose. God wants us to take care of our bodies and recognize the significance of our bodies as temples of the Holy Spirit. God lives in us through the Holy Spirit, and we dishonor Him by ignoring the value and importance of our own bodies. Look at it this way, we were bought at such a high price, that we sin against ourselves by having premarital sex. And God makes it plain in the Bible.

*Run from sexual sin! No other sin so clearly affects the body as this one does. For sexual immorality is a sin against your own body. Don't you realize that your body is the temple of the Holy Spirit, who lives in you and was given to you by God? You do not belong to yourself, for God bought you with a high price. So, you must honor God with your body.*

*1 Corinthians 6:18-20 NLT*

This is no easy command, but a must if we are going to properly honor God with temple in which we house the Holy Spirit. The world will not make this rule any easier to follow and neither will the men and boys that tempt us every day. But the same virtuous woman that is committed to her purpose can withstand any temptation. And why is this topic so difficult to discuss as among women, when so many, if not most of us have experienced it? God warns us about it in 1st Corinthians, so why not warn the young women around us. Build strength of mind in women and in numbers, so much that the devil will not even waste his time with tempting us. A sisterhood that protest sexual sin. Get our minds fastened and focused. When you are filled with Holy Spirit, you no longer belong to yourself and have been bought with a high price. God put value in your life and your body, gave up His only son. Now it's time we see the value of our lives and bodies as well. Hold ourselves out as the sacred, precious, artwork we were created to be.

Satan wants us so bad. Satan doesn't even need us to do wrong or sin. He just needs us distracted from God. It is not enough to just be a good person and live a good life. If you are not actively in engaged in a relationship with God, satan is happy. Yes, I said it. If you are distracted from God, satan is happy. If you are not focused on God, you are not fulfilling His purpose for you and you are aimlessly roaming through life without His direction. This means that you are not aggressively Kingdom building and this makes satan smile. If you are not committed to the work of Christ, satan is a happy camper. All satan needs is for us, as women to half-heartedly move about our lives, sidetracked from God and our purpose.

Distractions are a dangerous temptation. Distractions can come in any form and at any time. Distractions can be frivolous things that we do to fill our time or simply a lack of good time management. If we don't designate time with God, the same as we calendar time for everything else; well, everything else is the distraction. Just the same as television and shopping can be distractions, so can too much work and business in the house. Distractions can come by way of events that affect our emotions, leaving us responding in anger and hurt, rather than responding in peace. Satan spends his time drumming up ways to interfere with our joy in God. We reclaim our power from him by ensuring we are not tempted by his disruptions.

# CHAPTER FIVE

*I Thought I Knew it All*
*... I was Wrong*

We are not know-it all's. Why do we think we know it all? We believe it, so much so, that we will dismiss the opinions and suggestions of others at our own expense. In order for us to listen, sometimes we must get it wrong, go through a struggle or failure. By then, sometimes it's too late. A hard lesson learned to our detriment and for what logical reason? It was too painful to take the advice or heed the warning. Even more so, it's painful to hear "I told you so," or to say, "you were right." Why does it hurt so bad?

Have you heard of the term, "recreate the wheel" or "reinvent the wheel?" It's the idea of rebuilding, reconstructing something that has already been built and has a proven result. As young adults, we are the worst at rebuilding or repeating something that has an established history of consequences or failure, yet, we try it anyway. Why do we consistently repeat fads against sound advice?

We ignore good counsel, sometimes even against our better judgment. Wisdom would tell us to be more attentive when adults, guardians, and the experienced people around us provide us a few hints at life.

And God has a way of showing us daily that we could always use more wisdom. When the Bible talks about wisdom, it is not talking about being a Brainiac, being book smart, or having college degrees. You could spend your life ensuring that you know it all in that sense, but you must be prepared with Biblical wisdom in other ways. This scripture says it simply.

*The fear of the LORD is the beginning of knowledge,*
*but fools despise wisdom and instruction.*
*Proverbs 1:7 NKJV*

And the truth is that no one, but God, knows it all anyway. Unfortunately, we live our lives believing we have it all figured out. Have you ever thought something would go a certain way and it turned out completely different? Did you envision elementary school or middle school going one way and it went in the totally opposite direction? Most of the time, we are wrong, and we certainly cannot predict the future. Has your circumstance ever turned out differently than expected and it work out to your benefit? So much so that you were thankful that it did not go the way you planned. God can and does bless us much more than we could ever imagine. We are totally clueless, especially in our young age, not only to what we need in life, but also who we are and what we want. And if we are still learning who we are, how could we possibly plan out our lives without knowing more.

God wants us to gain our wisdom from Him, from scripture. The more you read it, the more it gets etched in your mind and heart. When you get into situations, life can send you into depression, peer pressure, loneliness, but you can pray on and recite those words of wisdom from memory. The Bible literally tells us that God's Word "is a lamp to [our] feet and a light to [our] path." Psalms 119:105 NKJV

Knowing the Bible will provide the light to your path. You don't have to know everything if you let God's Word direct your plans. The answers, the guidance is all there in black and white print.

Sometimes reading the words for the first time isn't enough, but when a situation arises, apply it and you will feel the power of God's words. The Bible is full of scripture that directly tells us how God will step into any situation and guide us.

In Acts Chapter 9, we learn the story of Paul on the road to Damascus. Paul thought he knew it all too, until the Road to Damascus. Paul, prior to his conversion to Christianity, intensely persecuted followers of Jesus and tried to destroy the church of God. Despite his exhaustive attempts to stop the spreading of the word and gospel of Christ, God still showed Himself to Paul. Paul despised Jesus and everything He stood for and this was after Jesus had already been crucified.

So, imagine this, Jesus has given His life for our sins and Paul makes it his life's work to spread hatred of Jesus Christ. Paul approved a killing of a young Christ follower and God still made a point to show Himself and shine through for Paul. He spoke directly to Paul in a way that only God could, and this let Paul know undeniably that it was Christ, Himself. Certainly, if someone hated you and acted toward you the way that Paul acted toward followers of Jesus, you too would have a hard time befriending Paul. In fact, you would probably try to avoid Paul and warn others about him. But that's what makes Paul's conversion to Christianity so great. Only God would make time for Paul to change. And if He's willing to make time for someone who publicly hated Him, can you even conceive what He would do for someone who is intently, with piercing focus, set on living the life God wants for us.

Everyone has their own Road to Damascus, a turning point when they realize, they really do not know it all and God is in control. And even in your worst circumstance, just like Paul, we can humble ourselves and change for the better. This is what it takes to fiercely represent and fearlessly trust in God.

# CHAPTER SIX

## The Bible is Better than Reality TV Shows

Reality check on reality television. How much time are we going to spend watching others live out their life? As fun and interesting as it may be, it is time lost developing our own purposes and destiny. Television series can be somewhat addictive. We get caught up in these intense stories and we can't wait to see the next week. Producers have a way of keeping us intrigued week to week, and season to season. How many shows do you keep up with each week? Even fictional shows create the same intense compulsion to watch each week. Just think about the conscious way we set our DVRs (digital video recorders), the intentional way we make sure not to miss a show, discuss with our friends and colleagues. We have open discussions about what happened in the previous show, what we think will happen in the next week. We have watch parties with friends and plan to watch together. What if we shared the same passionate commitment to plan, discuss, share, and discuss the Bible? We can learn so much more about God's will for us by reading the Bible. And believe it or not, there are equally interesting stories in the Bible.

We watch a lot of television and never have enough time to read the Bible. This is unfortunate because the Bible is exactly what we always need. Instead of spending every evening or night binge watching our favorite shows, we can "binge read" the Bible. Television can be hard to walk away from or stop watching. No need to give it up completely. I love a good television series as much as anyone. There is certainly a place for entertainment like television, movies, and sporting events. All these things are fun and exciting and create a way for us to temporarily step out of our lives and focus on something other than ourselves and our problems. Entertainment even helps when we just need to relax after a busy day at work or school. However, we can do the same thing by reading and studying the Bible. There are multiple ways to do this. We can simply read the Bible, we can read other Bible based books, applications, and studies. There are options for engaging in different types of entertainment and equally there are options for studying the Bible. What you will surprisingly find is that the Bible is more interesting, filled with troubled characters, battles, famine, disease and replete with characters with varying degrees of relationship in Christ.

Many of the characters, of course, were women, some Sheroes (female heroes) in their own right, some strong devout Christians, and others who succumbed to their temptations. Each of them, no matter what their life evolved into, are examples to us. Some Sheroes stood out in times when it was uncommon for women to do so. Some models of the Christ filled life we should live and others with less pleasing characteristics, but we can learn from them, nonetheless.

Let's look at Rachel. How many of you would be interested in a reality show that included romance, heartbreak, deception, scheming, theft, infertility, surrogacy, sibling rivalry, realized dreams, and a tragic end? Who would ever expect this to be all in one show? Meet Rachel. Rachel was a shepherd girl, and it was her responsibility to draw water from the well for her father, Laban's sheep. On what seemed a normal day for her, she approached the well, having already caught the attention of Jacob. Immediately smitten with each other, Rachel ran to tell her father about Jacob. A little background on this, Jacob was sent to Laban by his father, Isaac, and was a relative of the family. Jacob, prior to meeting Rachel, during his travels had a vision from God, detailing how God would bless him and his descendant. He vowed then to serve God with His promise of provision.

Jacob quickly asked Laban for Rachel's hand in marriage. Laban agreed, but only after Jacob worked for him for seven years. However, when Jacob completed his seven years of work, Laban offered him Leah, his older daughter, for marriage. Just imagine the despair Jacob and Rachel must have felt. But having no other choice, Jacob accepted and thereafter agreed to work another seven years to have Rachel the love of his life. This deception, all started by Laban, created competition, jealousy, and a rivalry between Leah and Rachel. And although Jacob, did not love and look at Leah in the same way he loved Rachel, she was able to have children. Rachel struggled with this and was extremely jealous of Leah. Leah on the other hand believed having children would bring Jacob closer to her. Leah eventually had four sons for Jacob. This made Rachel extremely jealous, but instead of continuing to wait on God, Rachel offered Jacob her hand maid Bilhah. Bilhah had two sons from Jacob, but this tormented Leah. Leah responded by giving Jacob her servant Zilpah to bear children for him. Zilpha eventually had two sons for Jacob. Rachel, still unsatisfied with infertility, then made a deal with Leah, that she could sleep with Jacob, if she shared some mandrakes, fruit she believed would help her to bear children. Leah agreed.

It seems the one thing Rachel had that no one could take away, was the love Jacob had for her and how much he favored her over all the women. However, in her attempts to please him, she agreed with Leah that she could sleep with Jacob. From this, Leah then had two more sons and a daughter with Jacob. For years, the sisters competed for love, affection, and to prove their worth by bearing children. Rachel finally was able to bear a son, Joseph and felt vindicated, but still wanted more and asked for another son.

During all this time, years, Laban still had not released Jacob with his wives and children. Once again Jacob found himself trying to deal with Laban to be free. Jacob began planning for his departure, but he was met with resentment from Laban's sons. Laban cheated him, lowered his wages, but Jacob pressed on, and knew without a doubt that God had protected him from any harm. With agreement from Rachel and Leah to leave without Laban's approval, they set out toward the land God had promised Jacob. Laban, upset, tracked them down and confronted them about some stolen household idols. Jacob had no idea that Rachel had stolen from Laban. He told Laban he can look for them and let anyone who has taken them die. Jacob confidently knew he had served Laban well, without stealing, lying, or cheating, for twenty years, had worked beyond the fourteen years agreed for his daughters, but Laban greedily wanted more and cheated him. Rachel, on the other hand, stole from him, and was able to keep this hidden from Laban. In spite of this, Jacob and Laban make a covenant between them to respect each other, and for Jacob to care for his daughters. Rachel later and ironically, died during the birth of a second son.

This is a great example of how we create shambles of our lives when we take things into our own hands and don't trust in God. It also produces more hostility, jealousy, and most of all, hurt when we implicate other people. So, what can we learn from Rachel? Rachel's story started with heartbreak. Her own father stole the love of her life, cheated the man she loved and created a lifetime of rivalry between her and her sister. And by no means was any of this easy. Dealing with the infertility alone, was enough to send her spiraling down on an emotional roller coaster. But responding in jealously towards Leah, was not the answer. Leah was as much a victim to her father's schemes as Rachel.

Rachel spent her life jealous of Leah, but Jacob loved Rachel more. She expended her time complaining about being infertile and Jacob adored her, despite her infertility. Now, that is true love. Jacob couldn't possibly love her anymore. Rachel focused on what was missing, instead of the blessings. Even in the struggle we must know who has control. God eventually gave her what she desired, but Rachel spent a lifetime trying to control everything. Not only is her story intriguing enough for television, but we can learn from her and so many other women in the Bible. Another one of Jacob's daughters, Dinah, was kidnapped, raped, and her brothers avenged her wrong by slaughtering an entire town. All against Jacob's wishes.

Women in the Bible have incredible narratives that would shock and awe any audience. Deborah who is discussed in Judges Chapters 4 and 5, was the only female judge in the Bible. She served as a prophet, judge, military leader, and song writer. She was known for following God's leading and crediting God with all her insight and accomplishments. Not all the characters in the Bible stood for noble causes, many like Eve, as you will recall, are remembered for downfall, disaster, and sinister actions. Look at Delilah, who accepted money to aid in the downfall of Samson. She seduced Samson, making him believe she loved him, and he revealed the secret of his extra ordinary strength was in his hair. Delilah told the Philistines, who came in the middle of night and cut his hair, making him completely weak Samson. The Philistines then gouged his eyes out. Delilah shows the gravity and depth some will go for money. Delilah influenced Samson to reveal his gift from God. Eventually, Samson was displayed at a festival of 3,000 Philistines for amusement and to be made fun of. They laughed believing they had Samson beat, but in one last attempt to avenge them, Samson prayed, put his hands on two center pillars that held up the temple, which caused the entire temple to crash down into rubble on the Philistine rulers and all of the people. Delilah, while not mentioned in the Bible, thereafter, had bought complete ruin to her people for one cunning, evil seduction amounting to 1,100 pieces of silver. It shows the severity of feminine charm being misused malicious motives.

There is one thing you can be sure, no matter what role these women played, God had a plan for them and lessons He wants us all to learn from them. Chloe had a small, yet important role.

*My brothers and sisters, some from Chloe's household have informed me that there are quarrels among you.*
*1 Corinthians 1:11 NIV*

The woman Chloe is only mentioned in the Bible once. But in that short verse we learn that Chloe's household told Paul that there was a disagreement among the Corinthians. They couldn't agree on who to follow. Paul, now aware of this division, reminds them that God is the one who saves and that they were all preaching the same message. The lesson was that they need to follow God instead of putting their hope in men. Chloe's household played a small part in this, but it had a major effect. Had Chloe and her household not been in tune to what was going on and the need for everyone to be on one accord with God, Paul may not have been notified of this.

Everyone has a purpose, sometimes we play a major role in effectuating God's plans and other times, we play smaller roles. Each of those purposes, no matter the size, is a key factor in fulfilling God's script for our lives. Never underestimate where God has you positioned in life. He knows and orchestrates all the intricate details. Take pride in the small roles, this is likely a test for how you would honor God in much larger positions. Every day, every moment we have to effectuate positive God influence around us, should be taken intently with care. God put us there for a reason. God put Chloe in that place, in that moment for a reason. And no, we didn't hear the rest of Chloe's story in the Bible, but what pride she must have carried for not only noticing the division, but for speaking out about it. No different than, planning a movie script or a television show, every person in the cast is needed to make the storyline work. Every person plays a part in making life work. No matter how small your role now, God has precisely planned the next position in your life. The first smaller roles, the difficult ones, even tragic, heartbreaking roles are preparing you. You will be ready for the starring role when that time comes. You will be ready to fiercely represent and fearlessly trust in God.

The Bible is saturated with examples of Godly women. Like Ruth, who can show us loyalty and dedication. Ruth 1:16, 17 NKJV. The woman with the issue of blood, who will show us patience, perseverance, and trust in God. Matthew 9:20-22 NKJV, Mark 5:25-34 NKJV, Luke 8:43-48NKJV We can go on and on discussing women of the Bible. Our lives will inevitably be very different from all these heroines, but their stories are guidepost for us. By reading about them, imagining them in our day and time, we can etch in our hearts the meaningful ideas and principles that God wants us to live by. Imagine Delilah in this time, twentieth century using her appeal to get what she wants, to the dismay of all of those around her. Delilah would not be the woman I would befriend, knowing at any offer of money, she would not only plan my demise, but ensure it.

Same as with the scriptures found in Proverbs 31, God gives us women a multitude of standards to live by, and we will not learn those benchmarks by submerging ourselves in reality television, modern day drama, and the false perceptions created on social media. We must create a balance of independent thought, deep consideration of God's will for us with the available experiences and entertainments in life. Mirroring what modern society wants for us is not from God. Educating ourselves in the Word, intentionally walking within His will and authentic purpose for us as individuals is what God wants for us. Sure, we can enjoy all of life's pleasures, but never forget that just like the characters we watch, God has plans for you too.

# CHAPTER SEVEN

## Hardship is the Opportunity to Build

*She is clothed with strength and dignity,*
*and she laughs without fear of the future.*
*Proverbs 31:25 NIV*

S trong is the new pretty. Who are we kidding? Strong has always been the new pretty. King Lemuel's mother gave advise back then, in Proverbs Chapter 31, that continues to hold true today. She recognized then what would be valued most in a woman, and a pretty face, although glamourous would not always be enough. In fact, there's no mention of her appearance at all. The virtuous woman described shows through her life why she was more precious than rubies and why she could be trusted and greatly enrich the life of her husband. Proverbs 31:10-11 NKJV. And her worth had nothing to do with how she looked on the outside, her wardrobe, or her possessions. It has everything to do with how she carries herself, how she responds in conflict and adversity, and Who she puts her trust in.

Strong character and dignity are what will allow you to persevere through difficult times. And you don't grow in character without having experienced some things. Personal experiences will whether good or bad leave dents, remains on your soul. They leave you etched, often molding you to the person you become. However, we cannot allow the actual hardships we experience, even in the worst scenarios, dictate how we are molded or transformed. With God, we can control how this intimately affects us. The Bible tell us before we go through the struggle that we are going to be fine. We don't have to learn how to overcome the hard times alone. We just need to know what scriptures offer us comfort during those hard times. When we understand where our joy comes from, where our strength comes from, our happiness cannot ever be determined by the things that happen to us. We can be and should be happy despite it.

But now that you get the idea of this, does not necessarily make it easy to live this way. Life is beautiful and often difficult, if not brutal for some. With pressing issues like economic and financial division, lack of institutional access, racial injustice; life is not often fair. This is just the shallow surface of what some face every day. Personal and private life-threatening struggles like disease and famine, are encountered every day by strong women. Cancer. A tough topic for all of us and unfortunately, no stranger to any of us. I've lost and had more than enough hurt and heartache at the hands of Cancer. These are the times we struggle to say and do the right things to support each other and the ones we care about. And I'm not one often lost for words. No doubt, it's hard. Brutal. But these are the moments God is desiring for each of us to look toward Him. When you have lost all the fight, all the hope, and you have nothing left to put forth. God wants you to look to Him. In the moments when you are broken down mentally and physically to your weakest, that's when you turn to God. This is when you fiercely represent and fearlessly trust in Him.

But know that even in death, we do not have to cope with or suffer alone. God has not only provided and paved a way, but He is the Way.

*Seek the Lord and his strength; seek his face continually.*
*1 Chronicles 16:11KJV*

*The Lord himself goes before you and will be with you;*
*he will never leave you nor forsake you.*
*Do not be afraid; do not be discouraged.*
*Deuteronomy 31:8 NIV*

The persistent theme throughout the Bible is that no matter what you are going through, no matter how big or small, God is with you. One of the most beautiful scriptures that provide encouragement and relief in times of trouble, discord, and disappointment.

*Do not grieve, for the joy of the Lord is your strength.*
*Nehemiah 8:10 NIV*

*A cheerful heart is good medicine,*
*but a crushed spirit dries up the bones.*
*Proverbs 17:22 NIV*

Not only is this consistent with the premise of Proverbs 31, but it furthermore shows that your strength doesn't come from any daily experiences but rather entirely from the Lord.

*The Lord is my strength and my song; he has given*
*me victory. This is my God, and I will praise him – my*
*father's God, and I will exalt him.*
*Exodus 15:2 NLT*

*The Lord is a refuge for the oppressed,*
*a stronghold in times of trouble.*
*Psalm 9:9-10 NIV*

Imagine the silhouette of a woman, no particular facial features, or gestures, but that from the crown of her head, draped across her shoulders, adorned about her waist, and flooding down to the soles of her feet, are beautiful, but weightless garments of strength and dignity. Before starting her day, before brushing her teeth or reading her first email, she guards herself with the raiment of strength and honor.

How is this woman, while busy being a manager, realtor, seamstress, farmer, upholsterer, able to laugh without fear? How is this woman who is as busy as a woman could possibly be, able to hold it all together, and yet have time to laugh? How is she so firm in faith in times of sickness? She laughs because her future is in

God's hands. She has no fear because her hope is in Jesus. You don't have to be pretty, perfect, or refined to be loved by God. You can be fierce and fearless because God will be strong where we are weak. When you rely on God, he will give you the strength you need to endure.

Some of us strong Proverbs 31 Women don't come from perfect, happy homes. Your version of Vee will be unlike any other virtuous woman. Your experiences have etched and molded you in ways that God only wanted you transformed. However, it's up to you to decide if you will allow the hardship to positively make you or detrimentally break you. It's up to you to make Vee as virtuous of a woman as you want to be, flaws, setbacks, disappointments, and all. God wants us all there, there being the standard He has set for each woman alike. The hardships are testimonies of tears and triumphs that we should use to pass on to up and coming Vees. A celebration of the strength and dignity that God daily provides every woman to carry out her purpose. Fiercely represent and fearlessly trust in God. Vee grew into the virtuous woman, a God Spoiled Brat, and you will too.

15 years prior to the Christmas party, if you look back, Vee was a quiet, shy girl. She came from a small family; two siblings and a hardworking single mom. They didn't have much by way of finances or material things, but the small home where she grew up was filled with love and a mother who led by example. Vee watched her mother work, hours, and hours on end, both professionally and for the family, all without complaint. Vee had such an innate respect for her mother and what she did for the family, but she always hoped for more. Vee, wanted to elevate this hardworking, loving, altruistic virtuous

mother by influencing generations of legacies, creating a sisterhood of righteous women. A sisterhood with an unbreakable pact to live upright influential lives led by God, committed to a spirit of enriching, and nurturing the women and little women around them.

Fifteen years ago, Vee prayed for gifts and talents that would reclaim her time, money, and most importantly, relationships, to enjoy life and glorify God. It took her a while to see the vision, but once she captured and understood the vision that God has for women, Vee was dedicated to sharing it and living it. She no longer wanted to be quiet and shy about God. Vee experienced things, low income, loss of loved ones, loss of friendships, rejection, sickness, loneliness. She understood grief and sorrow. She understood disappointment. Those experiences didn't have to hold her down anymore. She now knew and had grown to appreciate that her joy and strength came from God.

Hardship is an unfortunate part of life. Everyone has difficulties. No one is exempt. Not even you. So, what can we do to overcome these struggles? How can we encourage others to push through to the other side of life's problems, misfortune, and loss? What does God say about hardship and trouble?

What was the hardest thing you have endured? Maybe the loss of a loved one. Sometimes this seems completely unbearable. Going through it you wonder; how will I ever get through this? And then time passes, although with a lot of agony, it slowly gets better. The pain has a way of strengthening us. So much so, that when someone else goes through similar hardships, we know how it feels, we can sympathize. How many of us, take the extra step and help others get through it by encouraging them, telling them the things we hoped others would say to us during our time of trial.

*These things I have spoken to you, that in Me you may have peace. In the world you will have tribulation; but be of good cheer, I have overcome the world.*
*John 16:33 NKJV*

As virtuous women we want to be gracefully stressed. Living in those moments of loss and disappointment are not easy. But clothed in our strength and dignity we can handle those intense moments with grace. Allow God to speak to you in those times of hurt and rejection. He wants to hear from us.

*The righteous cry out, and the Lord hears them; he delivers them from all their troubles.*
*Psalm 34:17 NIV*

We laugh without fear of the future knowing that God will rescue us. This is not always the rescue plan that we have in mind, but He will always rescue us. Therefore, it's important to seek Him earnestly and focus on fulfilling our purpose. If we are consistently walking in that purpose, we will leave and live out the legacy that God intended; one that will continuously serve others after we are gone. The victories that God intended will be served even in our pain and our suffering. And that's where we find our joy; by serving purposes greater than ourselves. In building God's kingdom.

Surprisingly, good friendships go through trials as well. It is especially hard on women to lose or break up with a good friend. You don't have to give up on tough friendships. You can nurture good relationships, walk away from bad ones, and still be the living influence that woman needs in either situation. Choose someone that will strengthen your relationship with Christ. This should be true for friendships, boyfriends, spouses. God will guide you through it. Maybe at that time it's not your season to be in close relationship with that person, but God will allow you to plant seeds in that person that one day will grow into a blooming relationship with God. And when that happens, your purpose through that relationship will be fulfilled.

God plans for us even when we don't. The hardships are a part of the plan. He needs us to grow and build from the trials to position us for the next step in his plan. We must change our thinking and praise Him, even though the struggles.

Have you ever gotten through something tough, stressful, and eventually realized how it altered your life and your thinking, to the extent that you were grateful for the struggle? Instead of being upset about the struggle, you are grateful, honored even that God put you through it. Ever wondered how you got through it, how did you make it to the other side of stress, heartbreak? But so glad you did. There is always an opportunity in hardship, to recover, overcome, conquer. God wants us to take those opportunities to get closer to him and then share through testimony what we experience.

*Journal*

Dear El Shaddai (God Almighty, all powerful, Psalm 91:1 NKJV),

I was twelve years old when I got baptized. I was the last one in my group of cousins that took the walk down the long wide church aisle at Mount Zion Baptist Church. I had so much anxiety about it. Mom was an usher, dad played the drums, and my little brother, seven years old at the time, was learning to play the piano. Everyone in my family was involved in the church service in some fashion. I would occasionally sing in the youth choir. But most Sundays I sat on the second to last row so that I could sit near my mother while she ushered. It seems as if all my younger cousins had been baptized and all my aunts and uncles would ask, "when are you getting baptized." I would shrug my shoulders and hope that they would soon change the subject. Then they would ask, "well don't you believe Jesus died for your sins?" I would nod, yes. They would then look at me in dismay, shake their heads, with a soft smile because I had not made that outward showing. Now, were they really frustrated with me? No. But that was the way I felt. Every Sunday I dreaded the call to discipleship. This was the time, the pastors asked if anyone was ready to confess that Jesus was their Savior and died for their sins. The Pastor and often the deacons would walk the aisle, making sure no one needed assistance making their way up the long wide church aisle. I stood in the back thinking maybe if I don't make eye contact, no one will notice me. I'm not sure why I had so much anxiety in those moments. Why was I so fearful of making that public confirmation? But it

was both serious and scary to me. I remember thinking, I'm twelve and you want me to give my life to God; you want me to be born again. And even then, I recognized the magnitude of what that meant. But I waited until I was ready, until God motioned me, and said, let's do this, together. I have spent my entire life in church. I have been in church since before I could walk. Sunday service, Vacation Bible School, Choir Practice, and every holiday program I had at least a minor part or line to say. I was saturated in Jesus. I still have/had lessons to learn. I still did not understand what it meant to have a relationship with God. It also took years for me to understand the importance of relationships within the church. Even though I spent all that time in church, spoon fed Jesus, church folks, even me, can be a lot to digest. Sadly, most of us won't admit that. Thankful that you are a patient God.

Take us one spoon full at a time, we mean well. Of course, I had to eventually take that first step, and make the public confirmation that I believed Jesus died for my sins. But that was only the beginning of the journey.

Love,

God's Spoiled Brat

# CHAPTER EIGHT

## Let's Put it into Perspective

Have you ever felt like you can't manage to stay happy for very long? Every time things seem to go great, they go right back down and depressing before you can even enjoy the bliss. You finally ace a test in a class you've been studying really hard for, mom finally allowed you to buy that dress you wanted out of your favorite store, the cute guy you like finally smiled your way (and it seemed totally promising). Of course, all those things are short lived, so when the next failure, disappointment, or ruined past time comes around, you are sulking, sad, and sometimes completely indignant. Not only are you annoyed that it didn't go your way. You're also angry, hurt, and sometimes beyond consoling. Someone said something rude, mean, or offensive to you and you are ready to go off the deep end. Maybe it was a friend, someone you trusted, and they told your deepest dark secret after being told not to, and this has left you feeling betrayed, alone, and without friends.

It's an emotional roller coaster and unfortunately, we put ourselves up for the rocky, up, and down unpredictable ride. We set ourselves up for the disappointment because all our hope is determined by objects, people, and circumstances. In other words, our happiness relies on things that are completely out of our control. Our happiness is often controlled by things we do not even need. If we put all of this into perspective are all these objects and circumstances as big as we make them out to be?

Instead, we should show appreciation for what we have, the people in our lives, our support systems. And if you feel you don't have someone, think hard because that person is there; a teacher, a pastor, a friend's mom or dad, librarian, or hey, maybe this book. Let this book inspire you to develop relationships with people who will feed positivity into you. Better yet, you create and maintain your own positivity.

Do you even understand the depth of God's love for you? Just think of the person in your life who means the most to you. Your brother, your sister, best friend, mom, dad, whoever that person is. Pause for a moment and think of them right now. Think of all the reasons why you love that person so much. Write down all those reasons.

How would you feel if one day that person was gone and to no fault of their own? They took the blame for something and it cost them their life. One day you and this person are hanging out and it comes out that you did this awful thing. The price to pay for this awful thing is death by crucifixion. When it came time for you to be crucified, your favorite person in the whole world said I will pay the price. Before you could say or do anything to stop them, the debt has been paid.

Now, consider the fact that this person who paid this ultimate price knew you personally and you knew and loved them. They sacrificed but had a significant personal relationship with you. Compare this to the sacrifice Jesus made for people He did not have one on one contact with any of us in the flesh. How amazing is it that He gave His life so that we can have relationship with Him for all eternity? He did this without hesitation, without having been asked by us, and without true appreciation for the sacrifice. Oh, how much must He love us. He died for us before we knew what His death would provide for us. When we didn't see it, He knew the plan the entire time and took our place. He did this all for love. This shows the importance and value He places on relationship.

*For God so loved the world that He gave His only begotten Son, that whoever believes in Him should not perish but have everlasting life. For God did not send His Son into the world to condemn the world, but that the world through Him might be saved.*
*John 3:16-17 NKJV*

Sometimes, you must encourage others first and build a support system for yourself and those around you. Start showing the love of Christ and you will see how far it will carry you. If you don't have a person to turn to, even more of a good reason to turn to God. Give Him the opportunity to transform your life. Take small steps in the beginning. Take one day, instead of feeding negativity into your mind, only compliment yourself. For every negative thought you have about yourself, feed yourself one statement of praise. Do this, day by day, until you no longer linger on the negative thoughts. Take this a step farther and send a message of kindness to one person, a new acquaintance, a longtime friend, or your parent. You can change the negative images, thoughts, and feelings surrounding you every day in the people around you and make someone else feel loved by one simple gesture.

Sure, sometimes I must reset. I must regroup and renew my thoughts. I must remind myself of who I am and who God wants me to be. I'm not positive all the time but having faith in God allows me to keep my hope in Him and not in myself, others, or social trends. He provides my foundation for who I am and my happiness. You want to stop being obsessed with and depressed about the superficial; you want to change your thinking and your mindset from Negative Nancy to Virtuous Vee, learn who you are in Christ. Learn who you are in Christ and carve it in your heart; never forget. You want to know the truth about yourself, learn it from the one who counts the hairs on your head.

*Indeed, the very hairs of your head are all numbered.*
*Don't be afraid; you are worth more than many sparrows.*
*Luke 12:7*

He literally counts the hairs on our head. He tells me exactly who I am in the Bible. Knowing Him and who I am in Him is where our happiness should come from. The rest, quite frankly, is out of our control. So, what does the Bible tell us about who we are?

The Bible tells you: You are a temple of the Holy Spirit.

*Or do you not know that your body is the temple of the
Holy Spirit who is in you, whom you have from God,
and you are not your own? For you were bought at a
price; therefore, glorify God in your body and in your
spirit, which are God's.*
*1 Corinthians 6:19-20 NKJV*

The Bible tells you: You are being refined.

*Being confident of this very thing, that He who has
begun a good work in you will complete it until the day
of Jesus Christ.*
*Philippians 1:6 NKJV*

The Bible tells you:  You are complete in Christ.

*And you are complete in Him, who is the head of
all principality and power.*
*Colossians 2:10 NKJV*

The Bible tells you: You are accepted by Christ.

*Therefore receive one another,
just as Christ also received us, to the glory of God.*
*Romans 15:7 NKJV*

The Bible tells you:  You are Holy and without Blame.

*Just as He chose us in Him before the
foundation of the world, that we should be holy
and without blame before Him in love.*

*Ephesians 1:4 NKJV*

This list goes on and on. If you just continue to delve into the Bible and hang on to the intricately chosen words that God has said about you, you will learn more and more about yourself. Each one of those is true, if you just accept and believe. These are the Bible verses that are etched on Vee's heart when she walks so confidently into that Christmas party or any room at all. She doesn't care if a single person in that room likes her shoes, her dress, or her hair. She knows that she is Holy and blameless before God, and with that, nothing else matters. Vee's boldness comes from her confidence in God, not from any strength or talent of her own. Fiercely represent and fearlessly trust in God. Vee knows that she can be bold and authentic because God is with her everywhere, she goes, in spirit, in her heart, and in her mind.

We are so much more than ever changing fashion trends, stereotypes, teenage fads, and social media post with selfie sticks. And hey! I understand, I was not born yesterday. Hearing it from mom, dad, grandma, or even pastors isn't always enough, if you hear about God from anyone at all. I cannot truthfully say that it worked for me either. I had to learn for myself by reading the Bible, investing the time to know what God says about me. Who does God say I am? Once I understood that, I could see my value in everything I did, even when I failed. In fact, I could see my value most often when I failed and made mistakes. God wanted me to learn through those setbacks, like Hurricane Katrina, that it was not the end of the road for me. I could grow past bad grades and a flooded house. I still had a good life. My dreams and goals could all still be accomplished, but I needed to set aside the "brat mindset;" crying and making myself sick over things out of my control and focus on God; how could I be what He needs me to be.

Have you heard of the phrase, "A good woman is hard to find?" It sounds cliché, but that is the way God wants it to be. Any woman that is worth her weight will be difficult to find. She sets herself apart from everyone else, in the way she carries herself, in the way she thinks, acts, even in the way she is motivated in life. She stands out from the typical because she is extraordinary. She cannot be found in normal hang out places or anywhere people would expect young women to be. She is in different places because she is busy, working, building, planning, processing, providing, and serving. She is a hard worker. She knows her God given purpose and is working to fulfill that purpose. This doesn't mean she cannot be in normal places, blend in when she needs to, or be relatable. She is always humble, never forgetting that God is in control. It only goes to show that she recognizes the shortage of time she has in life to be influential and make a positive impact. She spends her time setting goals and accomplishing them. And yes, there are lots of women like her; those that can set tasks for themselves and reach their aspirations. However, the virtuous woman is distinguished by what principles guide her and more importantly, the Spirit that guides her.

In other words, it is not her own selfish goals that dictate her steps in life. She does not miscellaneously choose what pet project she is aiming for next. She knows who she is in Christ, what talents He has gifted her with and intently listens to His direction for her next moves. Her goals are His goals. She knows this because she knows God and fears Him.

There are a few things that I had to grasp before I could even wrap my head around becoming a virtuous woman myself. There are three key components to successfully navigating the virtuous woman world. In fact, I never accepted that I could be a virtuous woman until some life lessons helped me to recognize these three important points.

# None of Us Were Made to Look or Be The Same

Write this down, highlight it, say it repeatedly, and commit it to your memory. None of us were made to look or be the same. Say it again. None of us were made to look or be the same. The Bible tells us this repeatedly. It could not be clearer that God wants us to accept our diversity.

*For we are His workmanship, created in Christ Jesus for good works, which God prepared beforehand, that we should walk in them.*
*Ephesians 2:10 NKJV*

*You saw me before I was born. Every day of my life was recorded in your book. Every moment was laid out before a single day had passed.*
*Psalm 139:16 NLT*

*God has given each of you a gift from His great variety of spiritual gifts. Use them well to serve one another.*
*1 Peter 4:10 NLT*

*You made all the delicate, inner parts of my body and knit me together in my mother's womb. Thank you for making me so wonderfully complex! Your workmanship is marvelous—how well I know it.*
*Psalms 139:13-14 NLT*

Every single woman has her own attributes, features, talents, and gifts. God did not make us to look the same, act the same, think the same, or even like the same things. God made us to be unique, to have our own style, to make our own choices, to wear our hair different, dance to different music. Imagine a world of women or young adult women that dressed and acted all the same. What a boring world we would live in. God wants us to take pride in our differences. Our differences are what make us significant. It's what makes us special. Those special differences are what God has equipped us with to accomplish His mission and His purpose in our lives.

## Virtuous Women Still Make Mistakes

Virtuous women still make mistakes. No woman is perfect. No man is perfect.

*If we claim to be without sin, we deceive ourselves and the truth is not in us.*
*1 John 1:8 NIV*

Go back and read Proverbs 31:10-31. It is not that she didn't make errors, it's just that when it came time to be remembered by those that loved her, worked with her; those that watched her serve, none of the mistakes mattered in the bigger picture. If you are burning the midnight oil by serving others, taking care of business, using your talents to glorify God, mistakes are the last thing on anyone's mind. The woman that is juggling all the things; school, sports, hobbies, work, home, friends, family; with a good heart, is accepted for who she is, not for mistakes she's made along the way. The difference between the virtuous woman and the spoiled brat that gets upset when things don't go her way, is that the virtuous woman takes the mistakes, the setbacks, the failures, disappointments, regrets with a smile on her face. Attitude is everything. She is not disheartened by the failures and mistakes. She keeps on pushing forward, stays positive throughout her endeavors. Give yourself a little room to fail, not even one of us is perfect.

## Baby Steps:
## Greatness Does Not Happen in a Day

It takes baby steps. Greatness does not happen in a day. Absolutely anything that you want to be good at will take hard work, determination, and discipline. Being a virtuous woman is no different. In fact, it will take even more hard work, determination, and discipline. Being a woman in this society is by no means easy. Growing up in this society is not easy. Working toward something that will bring you fame and money, because it has its clear benefits, is easier to set the time aside to work at. Working toward being the disciplined servant that God wants us to be, well that takes an entirely different mindset and work ethic, with an eternal benefit. It is conscious, intentional personal growth in which you are constantly feeding into yourself. It takes the kind of work investment that you do behind closed doors, that others won't see or applaud. This is different from the kind of discipline that goes into becoming famous and wealthy because most people won't have an initial curiosity in your growth in Christ.

*Give your complete attention to these matters.*
*Throw yourself into your tasks so that everyone*
*will see your progress.*
*1 Timothy 4:15 NLT*

*Your beginnings will seem humble,*
*so prosperous will your future be.*
*Job 8:7 NIV*

*Like newborn babies, you must crave pure spiritual*
*milk so that you will grow into a full experience of*
*salvation. Cry out for this nourishment.*
*1 Peter 2:2 NLT*

*And let us not grow weary while doing good, for in due*
*season we shall reap, if we do not loose heart.*
*Galatians 6:9 NKJV*

This kind of greatness takes personal awareness. You must spend some quality time learning what your strengths and weaknesses are, and how to use them. It takes personal acceptance of both your weaknesses and your failures. Once you recognize it, accept it for what it is. Somethings we can challenge ourselves and get better, some talents are just not ours to flaunt or boast about. That is quite alright. No one is great at everything. And with that, we each must have a willingness to change. We must be able to take this personal awareness and use it to grow into the best possible version of ourselves. And the crucial part will be to maintain patience with yourself and the process. Being the virtuous woman, that God wants us to be is a constantly evolving lifestyle. We will constantly be growing, making self-corrections, and striving to do and be what God wants of us. Patience with yourself will be key to consistent growth.

And here's the thing, if we are going to continue this path to a virtuous woman together, those three foundational principles are imperative. If we, and I do mean, you and I, do not accept those ideals, we won't believe we too can be virtuous women. I cannot look like, think like, act like any other person or woman in this world. Virtuous women face failure and make mistakes. No woman became a virtuous woman in a day, a week, even years. It is a process.

So, if it takes baby steps to be a virtuous woman, what is the first step? What is the first step to being the woman that God wants me to be? I need to know what God wants before I can snap my fingers to be just that. And then take this a step farther, how do I know what God wants? Well, lucky for each of us, he provided us with an instruction book, one that has words straight from His mouth, teachings straight from His wisdom and guidance. How often do you wish there were a book on each of life's milestones to show you just what to do?

You know, like the "For Dummies" series of books. And there's the good news! The Bible is like a Life Guidance for dummies. If you want to know exactly what God wants you to do in a situation, you pick up your Bible. The even better news is that the Bible is not just there for us when we get into tough situations. The Bible is there for us to continuously read and delve into to get to know God. It is there for us to study, to memorize, to carry in our hearts. You do that so when a day comes, in the spur of the moment you need guidance and a quick Word from God, you have studied and memorized so much so, that you know exactly what God wants you to do. You've read so much about God, His Words, His actions, His principals, you know God and are building a relationship with Him. The first baby step to becoming a virtuous woman is having a relationship with God.

Take that a step farther by using your relationship with God to build relationships with others, parents, family, friends. Start there. Let's not even talk about husbands and children yet. Single women can align with God and be virtuous. Young adult women can align with the characteristics of a virtuous woman. The traits of a virtuous woman do not depend on having a husband and a family. You can start being a virtuous woman today. You start by building your relationship with God.

When you are building a relationship with someone, what are some of the things you must do grow with that person? Well, you cannot have a relationship with anyone if you do not get to know them. You learn what they like, what they don't like, what they love and what they disdain. So, you build a relationship with God, by getting to know Him. You get to know God, by digging deep into your Bible and reading. The more you dig, the more you learn the power and authority you have in relationship with God.

# CHAPTER NINE

## All Things for the Good

God's plans always work together for our good. Believe it or not, even when it doesn't seem like it. God's will is perfect.

*And we know that all things work together for good to those who love God, to those who are the called according to His purpose. For whom He foreknew, He also predestined to be conformed to the image of His Son, that He might be the firstborn among many brethren. Moreover, whom He predestined, these He also called; whom He called, these He also justified; and whom He justified, these He also glorified.*
*Romans 8:28-30 NKJV*

Vee wasn't astonishing at the Christmas party because she was glamorously fitted with the best clothes and shoes. The people at the Christmas party are awestruck and captivated by Vee because no matter what she has on, how she is feeling inside, she walks into a room like she owns it. They are mesmerized because Vee knows something none of them know; that the key to owning the room, the failure, the setback is recognizing the importance of a relationship with the one being in control of it all; God. You want to own your circumstance? You want to captivate and influence the people around you? Own up to who you are in Christ and live like you know it is true. Fiercely represent and fearless trust in God.

*Let your light so shine before men, that they may see your good works and glorify your Father in heaven.*
*Matthew 5:16 NKJV*

This is the light they see in Vee. This is the light they so desperately desire. No one wants to be Vee, but they want to know what she knows about Christ, they want to feel what she feels about Christ. Vee recognizes her strength in Christ and everywhere she goes that strength shines through.

Fearing God isn't the same as being afraid or scared. It is whole heartedly giving great reverence, respect, admiration, and devotion to Him; without fail, without doubt.

*Fear of the Lord is the beginning of wisdom.*
*Proverbs 9:10 NKJV*

*And he said to man, Behold, the fear of the Lord, that is wisdom, and to turn away from evil is understanding.*
*Job 28:28 NKJV*

*The end of the matter; all has been heard.*
*Fear God and keep his commandments,*
*for this is the whole duty of man.*
*Ecclesiastes 12:13 KJV*

*And now, Israel, what does the Lord your God require*
*of you, but to fear the Lord your God, to walk in all His*
*ways, to love Him, to serve the Lord your God with all*
*your heart and with all your soul.*
*Deuteronomy 10:12 NKJV*

What are you waiting for? Life has started. Don't wait for diplomas, jobs, relationships, husbands, or children to be what God has called you to be. God is here now. Nothing Vee does in her life depends on anything or anyone. In fact, it is the exact opposite. Because Vee is living out her purpose in full confidence in the authority of God, many people and factors depend on Vee. What people would be missing out on blessings if Vee gave up striving to live out her life for Christ? What would her family forego if she failed to fulfill her purpose? What events would not take place if Vee said she didn't care? What assignments would not get done if Vee said she was not ready or said a particular assignment wasn't trendy enough? What duties would go undone if Vee's service depended on her mood or perception of others.

And although Vee is a wife and mother, her standards are the same as any single woman or young adult for that matter. God provides the same strength, the same promises, and equal relationship to every one of us. He has set the same standards and commandments. We don't have to wait to be wives and mothers to live out the commandments set out. And remember Vee fears the Lord and is a true God Spoiled Brat in her own right. She knows fearing and respecting God is wisdom and understanding. This does not mean she does not seek God for help and blessings. This also does not mean that she cannot cry out to God for deliverance from daily circumstances. She knows that "God will meet [her] needs according to the riches of His glory in Christ Jesus." Philippians 4:19 NIV. Vee knows from delving into her Bible "give, and it will be given to you. Good measure, pressed down, shaken together, running over, will be put into your lap. For with the measure you use it will be measured back to you." Luke 6:38 ESV Simply put, you must dish out what you want to come back to you. Bless others and God will bless you over and above anything you can do or imagine.

My mother emulated a virtuous woman my entire life. But the most trying times were during the time of my dad's heart transplant. She handled it with such grace, she made it seem easy. This was an incredibly scary time for my family. We were told my dad's heart was only pumping at 10%, and after years of having a pacemaker, even still, that he would be put on the transplant list. My mom's faith never wavered. She carried our family through the trial until it became a beautiful testimony. She prayed us through it. And many others as well. But in what was a very tumultuous time, God had a plan. Having gone through that experience, allowed me and everyone in my family to know that when you need God, He is always there. It is experiences like this one that help me to recall, "all things work together for good." Things do not always go as you want them to go, and you will have struggles and health concerns, but God wants you to show that you can rely on Him and His promises. He is not saying that everything is always good. He's saying that despite the bad, it will all work together for the good of those that love Christ.

Vee, like my mother, will still hold God to His promises, but she will not be the typical brat that allows circumstance to dictate her mood and existence. She will remain virtuous even when God says no to her request, but she also knows that "all things work together for good to those who love God, to those who are called according to His purpose." Romans 8:28 NKJV. Throughout it all Vee, you, and I, will remain virtuous, in fear of, and in admiration of God. The woman understands the difference between the monster child spoiled brat that cries every time things don't go their way, and the ever-reliant virtuous woman who is God's Spoiled Brat because she is a spoiled believer in His promises. This virtuous woman is spoiled by God in every sense of the word spoiled. This woman has inscribed on her heart, believes in her soul "if God is for us, who can be against us? He who did not spare His own Son, but delivered Him up for us all, how shall He not with Him also freely give us all things?" Romans 8:31-32 NKJV. She is God's Spoiled Brat because she knows when the perspectives of everyone else and social media created doubt about her self-image, abilities, and self-worth, that God spoiled her with praises of all the things she honestly represents. God told her she was a Temple of the Holy Spirit. God told her she is being refined. God told her she is complete. God told her she is accepted. God told her she is Holy and without blame. This virtuous woman is you, just believe. Fear God, he is ready to send you praises.

105

*Journal*

Dear Jehovah Nissi (The Lord is my Banner, Exodus 17:15),

Grateful during the trauma. I am so sorry that it took so long to love myself. Sorry that it took so much to appreciate the skin that I am in. I missed all the opportunities to enjoy and recognize all the small gifts you provided. Looking at myself today, and hopefully every day thereafter, pleasantly satisfied. I love every extra plump roll, that has initiated every diet and workout goal. I love the small space between my teeth that I've attempted to fix twice with expensive dental work. I love the large birthmark on the right side of my face, ever changing and ever growing with my age, even though I've considered facial treatments to remove it. I love my eyebrows that I fight with weekly to alter because they don't match; my hair and my slowly receding hairline; my feet and my oddly long toes. The list, if I continue to consider, can go on and on.

God, you flipped me upside down literally, emotionally, and mentally. Everyone has asked, how am I doing and how could I have possibly lived through an accident like this. I have given all the generic, expected answers, "I am truly blessed," "my angels were definitely surrounding me," "God just wasn't ready for me to go yet," "I'm so grateful no one else was in the car with me.", "I am so blessed to be alive, I don't have any complaints." But the truthful answer is that there is the me before the accident and the me after the accident. I had the normal residual effects of a traumatic car crash, nervous anxiety while driving or riding in a car, soreness from tensing my body during the crash, bruising from the seat belt, burn from the airbag. But then there are the spiritual aspects. It's amazing to me that it took something so potentially catastrophic to shape the rest of my life. I wouldn't want it to take anyone else this much or that long. God how can I help them get there, to her, the confident, yet humble, selfless, serving God fearing woman, but without the life-threatening crash.

Every awkward, ill shaped, thick curved, piece of me that you formed from dust, and in your likeness, that I've hated for so long; finally, finally receives the love and admiration, she deserves. I now know all the reasons to love it, myself, my soul, endlessly. Too bad it took a life threatening yet redeeming crash for me to sign off in approval. But ever so grateful for the crazy ride.

I lost control of my car after the tire blew on the interstate. Seconds later it overturned, possibly more than once, and landed right-side up. I prefer to call it an upturn, you will see why. The results of it have been more of a positive improvement for me than you would expect from a rollover car accident. And the fact that I landed right-side up; well, I like to think that my feet are better rooted and planted than ever before. I thought the anxiety about driving again would kill me, but it has only slowed my thoughts to consider more important things than always racing down the highway, or life, to get to the next thing or thought. I always moved too quickly. I had things to do and did not have time to slow down for thoughts, or anything. Life moved fast, so I did too.

This car accident was one of the scariest things I've ever experienced. Those seconds were the fastest, yet the longest seconds of my life. And still, in those moments none of the concerns that I have daily mattered then. What mattered, is that God protected me in every way possible during the time that I needed Him most. He was there. When I could do nothing, He did everything. It was as if he cleared a path for my huge vehicle to glide across the highway into and out of oncoming traffic while flipping over, I ran into no one and no thing ran into me. I landed right side up and in the most grateful, astonished way, I walked away on solid ground without a scratch or injury. I knew in those moments, when my feet planted, I had to show my appreciation through fulfilling my purpose. This book is just the start.

Love,

God's Spoiled Brat

# CHAPTER TEN

## Do it in Love

There are so many wicked and corrupt things going on in the world around us. Unfortunately, everyone you meet, or encounter does not have good intentions. But the good news, is that there are more of us that care about others, than those that lack compassion. The great news is that each one of us can spread more of that love and compassion everywhere we go. In fact, God says, it's our responsibility to do so. Jesus tells us in Matthew 22:37-38 NKJV that the first commandment is to love God with all your heart, mind, and soul. He then says the second most important commandment is to love your neighbor as yourself. The Bible tells us very blatantly that the greatest instruction from God is to love Him and love our neighbor. It could not be more simply said. Words straight from Jesus' mouth. There should be no hesitations or uncertainties about this demand.

*Jesus replied: "'Love the Lord your God with all your heart and with all your soul and with all your mind.' And the second is like it: 'Love your neighbor as yourself.' This is the first and greatest commandment.*

*Matthew 22:37-39 NIV*

And not only does God command us to love, but the Bible even further tells us that God is love.

*And so we know and rely on the love God has for us. God is love. Whoever lives in love lives in God, and God in them.*

*1 John 4:16 NIV*

*The very breath of God is in you. The Spirit of God has made me, And the breath of the Almighty gives me life.*

*Job 33:4 NKJV*

*The one who does not love does not know God, for God is love.*

*1 John 4:8 NIV*

*Love bears all things, believes all things, hopes all things, endures all things.*

*1 Corinthians 13:7 ESV*

If God is love, and God lives in us, then we are love. So, when the Bible tells us love bears all things, we can bear all things; you can bear all things. You can believe all things, hope all things, and you too can endure all things - weight gain, money problems, relationship failures, bullying, bad grades, loneliness, fear, anxiety, image issues, peer pressure. Nothing is exempt. You can endure and overcome because God has overcome the world.

*I have told you these things, so that in me you may have peace. In this world you will have trouble. But take heart! I have overcome the world.*

*John 16:33 NIV*

With that, be empowered. Carry that power you have in love with you everywhere you go. Without love you are nothing, but with it you can have, do, and overcome everything.

How do you spread the love of Christ? How can we become doers of His word? Simply by being the virtuous woman He has equipped each of us to be. We do this by being committed to our purpose each day. We spread the love by following the guidance in Proverbs 31. To show love you have to be the woman that people trust, that works hard, diligently through day and night, cares for others and her household, carries herself with dignity, only speaks with wisdom and kindness, and most of all, and above all, reverences God. If you are consistent in this, taking each day, even in the difficult moments, with God in your heart, you will be sharing God's love without hesitation, without reservations. By walking in the purposes that He has for us, we will be fierce disciples of Christ. Modeling the image of a woman that God planned for each of us.

But we need to take this a step further, beyond just exhibiting virtuous woman qualities, and that of a God's Spoiled Brat. We must develop the women around us, transforming our local communities of women into God's Spoiled Brats. Every woman can take on small projects of support and mentorship. Don't overthink this to be huge missions or developments with large groups of people. All you need to do is be more intentional about the relationships and women around you. Be purposeful. When you are around family and your younger impressionable female cousins, take time to talk about God and His intentions for us. Introduce them to Vee and tell them what it means to be God's Spoiled Brat. Use your life experiences and Godly gained wisdom to prepare them for all the things to come in life. Allow them to gain the wisdom some of us have sought for years in normal interactions with you. They will see God's Spoiled Brat in the way you live, the way you speak, and most of all in the you share your insight and fear of the Lord.

The mini-God Spoiled Brats deserve to look at women like Vee, that have experiences and testimonies to share. Women and young girls just like you. The world needs empowered women of God, that live life by His standards and with wisdom from His word to leave impressions on younger generations. Sooner rather than later, of course. And there is no age requirement to start. If you love God, have a relationship with God, it's time. It is time. Time to plant seeds for new growth in Christ among women. It is time to strengthen the sisterhood.

Look at Mark Chapter 4 and The Parable of the Sower. Not only does Jesus tell us to take opportunities to sew seed wherever we go, but He also wants us to accept

112

people for where they are in life. We can be intentional about planting the seeds, God will initiate the growth.

*So, neither the one who plants nor the one who waters are anything, but only God, who makes things grow.*
*1 Corinthians 3:7 NIV*

*The sower sows the word.*
*Mark 4:14 NKJV*

Mark 4:14 says, "the sower sows the word." When we do our part, God will do the rest. Yet again, the Bible has the answer. He gives you exactly what you need. His words, His promises, and reading, learning, studying, and finally experiencing the Bible will help to engrave Him in your heart. You will learn and know Him by knowing His Words. You experience the Bible by applying it to your life. Uttering His Words when you need them and holding them safe in your heart for use exactly when you need it. Let His words be your comfort when troubles have you stressed. Allow Bible scripture to be your wisdom, your guidance when you are lost from the path.

*Blessed be the God and Father of our Lord Jesus Christ, the Father of mercies and God of all comfort, who comforts us in all our tribulation, that we may be able to comfort those who are in any trouble, with the comfort with which we ourselves are comforted by God.*
*2 Corinthians 1:3-4 NKJV*

And here is the big truth, that can be rather simple, if you believe it in your heart. 'If you openly declare that Jesus is Lord and believe in your heart that God raised him from the dead, you will be saved. ' Romans 10:9 NLT It says you WILL be saved, not maybe. This is a promise from God.

*Seek the Kingdom of God above all else, and live righteously, and he will give you everything you need.*
*Matthew 6:33 NLT*

We also know now that God, Jehovah Nissi, is our Banner. God will stand before us. He will provide. He will protect. However, without the circumstance, without the hardship, you would never know what you can accomplish and overcome with God. How could Moses have ever known that with a rod he could part the red sea, if he never trusted God. How could Moses have ever known that he could defeat the Amalak army with a small army of former slaves, if he did not trust in God. Exodus 17:15 NIV It's the hardships that provide us with the chance to build our character, to know exactly what we can do. Now, would I ever have asked God to put me through a terrifying car accident to get to where I am with my relationship with God; of course not. I also would not want anyone else to experience it either. However, whatever event is put before us, with focus on God and His purpose for us, we can alter a bad situation and completely turn it around for our good. And that is the key, to keep moving F.O.R.W.A.R.D. Focus On Righteousness with A Renewed Determination. (Author Unknown). If you are always moving and thinking forward, you get to start fresh with a renewed spirit. You should even pray for that specifically.

*Create in me a clean heart, O God;*
*and renew a right spirit within me.*
*Psalms 51:10 KJV*

Just remember to start building the sisterhood and building confidence and influence in other women, you must develop as an individual as well. When it gets tough, don't forget the three essentials you learned in Chapter 8. None of us were made to look or be the same. Virtuous women still make mistakes. Greatness did not happen in a day.

It takes a village. You can't learn how to be a virtuous woman all on your own. You need God, first and foremost, support from all the beautiful, hardworking, God fearing women in your life. Engage in a small group or Bible study; grow together.

*Let the message about Christ, in all its richness, fill*
*your lives. Teach and counsel each other with all the*
*wisdom he gives. Sing psalms and hymns and spiritual*
*songs to God with thankful hearts.*
*Colossians 3:16 NLT*

And if you can't find one nearby, you inspire the village around you, share the book, share the guidebook, spread the word, inspire the change you want to be and create. We are all learning along the way. So, balance the circumstances and obstacles before you, God hears you, God loves you, and will help you overcome with grace and class, just like Vee. You will persevere with strength and dignity just like a virtuous woman; just like a God Spoiled Brat. You must choose to do it all in love. You choose, to fiercely represent and fearlessly trust in God. Beauty fades, fashion evolves, friendships fail, and people change, but a woman who fears the Lord will always be celebrated.

*A special thank you to the people and businesses who have played a part in the writing and production of this book.*

*God's Spoiled Brats, LLC.*
*www.godsspoiledbrats.com*

| | |
|---|---|
| Kennisha Griffin | @createandblossomllc<br>www.createandblossomllc.com |
| Tyra Nicole Dumars | www.tyranicole.com |
| Damontre' Guiton | @coop_gon_work |
| William Minix,<br>Author, Consultant | "Leadership: Why Managers Fail?<br>10 Mistakes to Avoid When<br>Managing People" |
| Kelly Hornberger | @kellyhornberger<br>www.kellyhornberger.com |
| Saumatic Sessions | @saumatic_coop |
| Tammy Harper | www.flawlessenvymakeup.com |
| Jasmin Monroe | @sheisjmonroe |
| Erik Quinn | @onecreativehtx<br>www.onecreativehtx.com |
| Mari Balentina | @madee_b<br>linkedin: Mari Balentina |

| | |
|---|---|
| Skylar Grace Spas | @skylargracespas |
| Cha Cha's Creations | @chachascreations16 |
| Bertha LeBeauf, Evangelist, Mentor | |
| Janay Fournette, Author | "What to Do When You Don't Know What to Do" |
| Steven Fuller | www.sdgraphix.com |

GOD'S *Spoiled* BRATS